Raised by Dick and Jane

From Fantasy to Reality:
A Mom's Musings on Motherhood

Maureen George

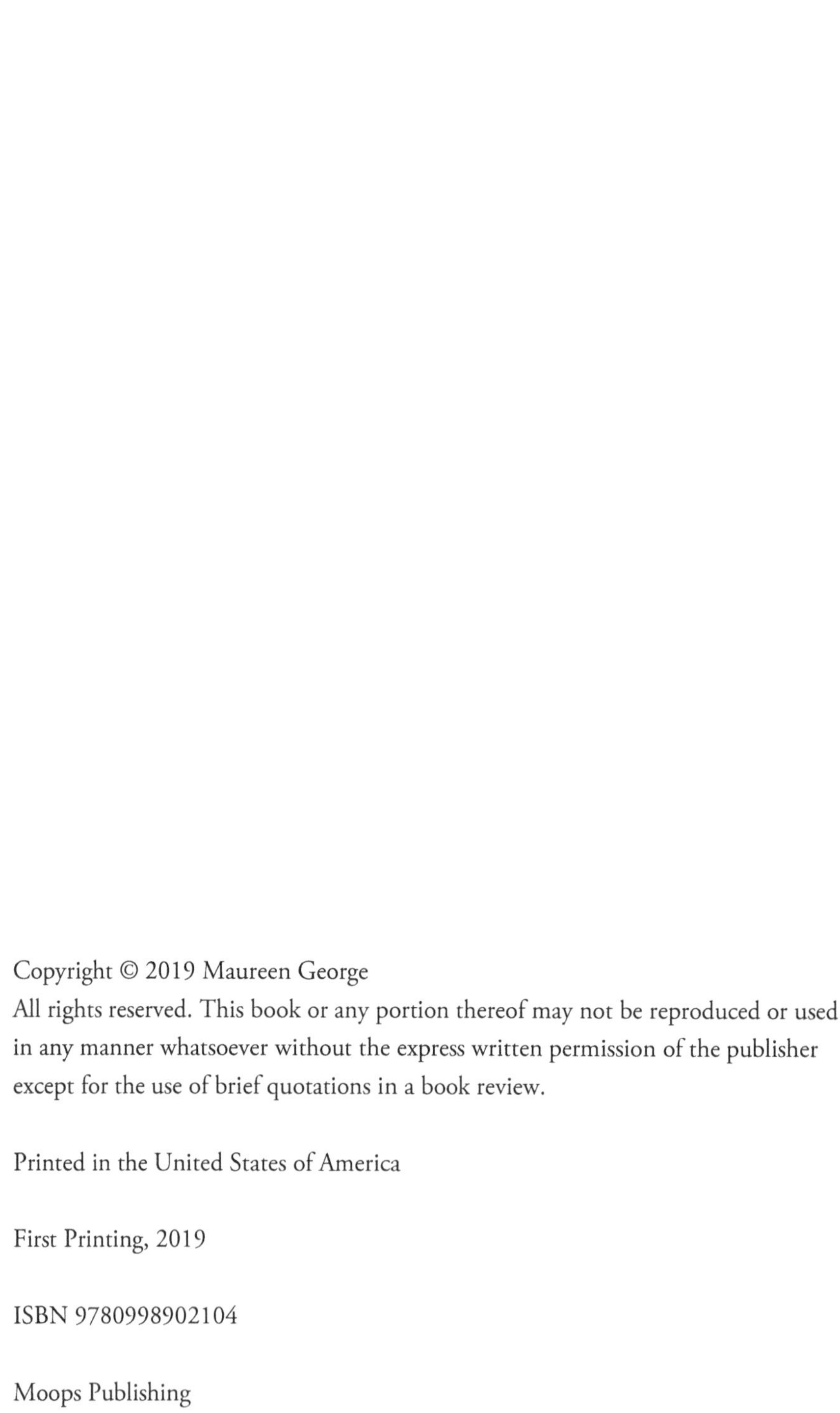

Printed in the United States of America

First Printing, 2019

ISBN 9780998902104

Moops Publishing

To Zachary and Alex, for making me a mother. You are two of the most interesting, talented, intelligent and dynamic young men I have ever met. Thank you for teaching me how to be a good, hopefully, but at least proficient mother.

To David, my loving husband, for making me a mother –
I couldn't have done it without you.
Thank you for all of your love, support and humor
through this journey of parenting.

Contents

Preface

After writing this book and contacting literary agents, the question came up of why I wrote it in the first place. Following is the answer.

As my dad's name was Dick and my mom's name was Jane, I was literally raised by Dick and Jane, the names of the two beloved characters of children's books known the world over. But mine was hardly a storybook childhood.

For instance, I looked forward to living with my mom during high school, after living with my dad and two brothers for a few years following my parents' divorce. It would be nice to have some female companionship.

Or so I thought.

Instead, it proved to be a tough time. For example, I spent many evenings alone and sometimes got locked out of my house with no way to reach my mom. On those days, I would sit outside on a bench after school and try to do my homework until it got dark. If I was lucky enough to have some money, I would walk to a nearby liquor store to buy some nuts for dinner. Otherwise, I went without. When it was finally evening, I would knock on a neighbor's door and ask if I could spend the night. I hated that - it was very embarrassing and felt like I was begging.

When I became a mother, I threw myself into motherhood because it was so important to me. I yearned to be a much better mom to my two sons. Years into my experience, I started writing this book. But this is not a "woe is me" tale. Being an eternal optimist and having a good sense of humor, I wrote this book in a lighthearted tone.

Raised by Dick and Jane is a compilation of relatable, amusing anecdotes regarding the trials and tribulations of motherhood that moms, from newbies to seasoned veterans, can identify with. It has brief chapters that are easy to read, like:

- *Whew! Thank God it's Monday!*
- *Cooking Used to Be One of My Hobbies*
- *Mom, What's the 'F' Word?*

Coming from the framework of being "raised by Dick and Jane," I interspersed some "Dick and Jane Moments" at the end of select chapters. These are flashback memories of quirky parenting moments from my childhood that relate to that particular chapter.

Raised by Dick and Jane doesn't try to teach moms how to be the best mothers or debate about which culture has superior parenting skills. It's written in an irreverent and sometimes reflective tone, which is inclusive of all moms' experiences.

The world of motherhood can be exhausting and downright overwhelming at times, but it is also a most important and fulfilling calling. These ruminations aim to entertain the reader in a fun, positive way and really, can't we all use a little "feel good" in our lives?

I hope you enjoy!

In the Beginning …

Pregnancy

Well, you pee on the stick and after about 15 minutes you see two lines or a plus sign or whatever indicator those home pregnancy tests now use. And you're so excited because you've been waiting for this moment (I'm assuming you have if you're reading this book.) So, this is how it all begins – the 9-month long journey into becoming a mother.

With my first pregnancy, my husband would wait with me after I peed on the stick. It took quite a few months and we were used to disappointment, so when the stick showed I was pregnant, we were so excited! Then I called my OB/GYN to set up an appointment to make sure. He mentioned that the home pregnancy tests are nearly 100% correct when they give positive results. It's their negative results that could be wrong. So, I went to my appointment and the stick was correct – I was pregnant!

When I found out I was pregnant with my second child, I again peed on a stick. But this time my husband wasn't waiting with me. In fact, he didn't even know I had peed on a stick. I just did this because I missed my period and before I called to make an appointment with my doctor, I knew he was going to ask if I had taken a home pregnancy test. I knew I wasn't pregnant yet. I had just gotten off the pill and this was the first month. It had taken many months with my first pregnancy and I thought it would take longer for the second one because I was a bit older. So imagine my surprise when I got a positive result! I knew it was right because of what my doctor told me before.

We were trying to get pregnant, we just didn't realize it would happen so quickly.

So, I put the stick on a towel on our bed and nonchalantly went downstairs and asked my husband, David, to go up to our room to get something. He grumbled, but went up. Then he came downstairs with a shocked smile on his face. As I was standing there holding our 11 month-old baby, he said "are you pregnant?" I said "yes"! We were so excited, but very surprised!

For the first pregnancy, I bought all the books and magazines regarding pregnancy and parenting that I could. I sucked up as much information as possible. I ended up getting horrible morning sickness. They call it morning sickness, but it was a misnomer in my case because it lasted *All Day Long!* It got so bad, I could barely eat anything. I would try to chomp on a few crackers and sip some water. There would be days where I was lying down all day long, only getting up to move from the bed to the sofa and to go to the bathroom. Even on days when I felt pretty good and decided to go out and get as much done as possible, the waves of nausea could overpower me at any time, to the point where I needed to go home to lie down or find a bathroom to get sick in as soon as possible.

One such incident happened one day while I was Christmas shopping. I stopped at a café to get a bowl of soup. I thought it would be nice and light and good for me. I ordered butternut squash soup. It sounded good. When it arrived, it looked good. When I first tasted it, it tasted good. However, after a couple of bites I had to get out of there. FAST! For some reason I got uncontrollable waves of nausea. To this day, I cannot eat butternut squash soup.

Another incident happened one evening when David and I tried to go out to dinner. We went to a restaurant where I could get roasted chicken. Something simple that would be easy on my troubled stomach. I ordered a festive, non-alcoholic drink of cranberry juice and sparkling water. For some reason, that drink set me off. We had to pack up the chicken and leave. To this day, I haven't touched cranberry juice.

Don't even get me started on coffee. Before pregnancy, I always loved coffee. I'm the type of person who buys the whole bean variety and grinds it right before brewing it. I liked Starbucks so much that I eventually bought stock in the company. If I was going to be spending so much money there, I might as well get something back from them besides really good coffee. Well, when I was pregnant, the mere whiff of coffee would send my stomach churning. It was like Syrup of Ipecac to me. It could instantly cause me to get sick. My poor sister-in-law visited us during this time period. She couldn't make coffee at our place, so she went out one morning to buy some. She was sitting in another room sipping it, but I could still smell it and could barely contain my nausea. Thank God for the second trimester, when the nausea finally went away. Although it took me a couple of months after giving birth for me to be able to drink coffee again.

I never got morning sickness with my second pregnancy and even drank decaf coffee! It just didn't repulse me the way it did the first time around. Funny thing about pregnancy – each one is different. In fact my second pregnancy was easier than the first, probably because I knew what to expect. Although, I got sick with an awful cold that turned into bronchitis during the last trimester and it lasted a couple of months. I had such a hard time sleeping because I couldn't stop coughing. I would sleep on our sofa so I could try to sit up because lying down made the cough much worse. But I always had a hard time getting to sleep and would wake up continuously throughout the night because of the coughing. My doctor wanted to give me codeine and said it was safe to use during pregnancy, but I didn't want to take it because you always hear of new medical studies that come out and find that something was much more toxic than we previously thought, especially with fetuses and young children. So I just did as best I could, even though I was working full-time at that point.

But I did love being pregnant. It was just so exciting to know that a person was forming and growing inside you. I felt love for both my babies right away. It was so exciting to hear the first heartbeat and then the first ultrasound just takes your breath away! I was nervous during the ultrasound and other tests because you're waiting for confirmation that everything's OK and I've known people who hadn't gotten good results. We were lucky and we're very grateful.

Once the babies got old enough to move around and start kicking, it is so exciting!! There would be times when David and I were sitting in bed and the baby would start kicking. So, I would put David's hand where I could feel the most kicking and he would feel it! Once, we actually saw something move across my abdomen. Whether it was a hand, foot, arm or leg, we'll never know. But it was strange, cool and a little freaky – a bit like the movie "*Alien*".

So, as you're nearing the 9-month point, you start to get really big and uncomfortable and ready for the next stage: childbirth. One final point, though. We didn't want to find out the sex of our babies until childbirth. There are so few good surprises in life, as David would say. So, part of the drama of childbirth would be the anticipation of finding out whether we had a son or daughter. Now on to the next chapter …

And Childbirth

We took childbirth classes during my first pregnancy. Again, I read as much information as I could get my hands on. One thing that gets mentioned in these classes and a lot of the material I read is a birth plan. Doctors must hate birth plans. I dutifully devised my birth plan and discussed it with my doctor, who, bless him, patiently listened to my ideas on how I wanted my birth process to go without erupting into laughter. Now, maybe some women actually get nice, well-executed birth stages that go as planned, but for the rest of us, Mother Nature does what she wants and guffaws at our well laid-out intentions.

With my first pregnancy, I got sick during my 36th week of pregnancy. I hadn't been feeling real great for a few weeks before that but I thought it was usual since I was nearing the end of my pregnancy. One thing David, my family and I noticed was that I seemed to be looking really bloated, especially my ankles and feet. They got so big that they didn't even look like they were supposed to be part of my body. David even took a picture of them because they were so swollen.

A couple of days after we noticed this, I started to get really nauseous and vomit. It got to the point where I couldn't keep anything down, not even water. This happened for a few days and I was in contact with my doctor's office each day. They finally had me come in and my urine test detected protein in the urine and my blood pressure was elevated. So, my doctor had me get a blood test. I was lying on my sofa on a Friday morning when I was feeling so sick, I decided to call the doctor's office to see if the results had come in. He checked and told me he was admitting me into the hospital, so I needed to pack up. He said he would have our baby delivered around the end of the day.

When I got to the hospital, my birth plan was thrown out the window when I started going into labor and my baby started showing signs of fetal distress. They called my doctor to tell him to get to the hospital right away and I was whisked into the operating room for an emergency C-section. Turns out I had developed pre-eclampsia and I had a dangerous form of it called HELLP syndrome. Thank God, my son, Zach, and I were alright. I later learned that the doctor told David that fifty years ago, he would have lost both of us. That day I learned the only thing that matters is that a healthy baby is delivered. How that happens is icing on the cake.

Our second child, Alex, was delivered about a year and a half later via planned C-section. We weren't going to take any chances this time. We had learned that there is an increased risk of uterine rupture when a woman with a previous C-section tries a vaginal birth and the risk increases more because this birth was less than two years later. We knew from experience that things can go south quickly, so we just weren't going to take any chances – we were playing it safe this time. This birth experience was much calmer and we got to welcome our second son into the world with a roomful of family and friends.

Why Won't They Stay Asleep?

After Zach was born, David and I adjusted to life with a newborn, or we tried to. People warned us toward the end of my pregnancy to try to get as much sleep as possible because sleep would be precious once the baby came. No one can prepare you for how true this is! First, newborns need to eat about every two hours, day and night. Their small stomachs just can't hold much food and they are growing and developing so rapidly that they need constant fuel. David would take one of the shifts in the middle of the night to help me out and he helped whenever he was home. He was working full-time so it was hard. But I needed some help, as any new mother will tell you, because I was so consistently sleep-deprived day after day.

The night and early morning schedule looked like this in the beginning: baby eats at 10pm, midnight, 2am, then 5am. Then it was about every two hours after that. The baby would last from 2am to 5am for some reason and we were grateful. I would usually do the 10pm and midnight feedings, then my husband would do the 2am feeding. We would both always wake up when it was time for a feeding because the baby's crying was so loud. By the time he was fed and his diaper was changed, it took about a ½ hour. So if I was doing the next feeding, I would only get 1 ½ hours in between if I fell asleep right away. Sometimes I would stress out about that and not be able to fall asleep right away.

At one of our pediatrician visits, the doctor asked us if Zach was sleeping through the night and we told her his schedule. She told us to hold off his last feeding until about 11pm and then to not feed him again until 5 or 6am. So when he would wake up and cry around 2am, just let him cry it out until he fell back asleep. I was aghast! Let a 4-week old cry it out in the middle of the night when he feels like he's starving?! My instinct told me this was wrong but I was a new mother, so I didn't feel confident my instinct was right. I mean, the pediatrician is telling me this. She takes care of children for a living and said she did this with her own children. I left that office appointment and started crying because I was so conflicted and didn't know what to do. I also didn't like her demeanor during the visit. She seemed cold, not warm and caring, and that upset me.

I talked this all over with David, who was also at the appointment, and we decided we needed to get another opinion and decided to talk to other pediatricians. We visited two other pediatricians and I talked to a few moms, who ended up agreeing with David and me, and we found a doctor we liked much better. He told us to stay on our schedule, but to try to push the feeding times apart little by little. He said that a 4-week old is not expected to sleep through the night. Their stomachs aren't large enough to hold enough food for six hours or more. He let us know that we just needed to be patient and in time the feedings would extend from about 10pm to about 6am (heaven!) This happened around 4 months old and it was a natural process that wasn't exceptionally painful for baby or parents.

So, this is what happens when they're babies. But your sleep troubles aren't over once they leave the baby stage. For both of my sons, once they moved from the crib to a "big boy bed," they discovered very quickly that they could get out of bed. So the constant interruptions of "I need more water," "I need to go to the bathroom," "can you sing another song?" "what are you doing?" etc., etc. began. Finally, this started to curtail as they moved into school-age, although then the problem became getting them to fall asleep.

Crawling vs. Walking

Your babies inevitably get to the stage when they start crawling. And very quickly, they learn how to crawl at lightening speed. Before you know it – zoom! – they're moving from room to room and getting into things faster than you can turn around.

I must admit, I was not a big fan of the crawling phase. Before that, you could contain them in one area and they needed you to move around. So you could turn your attention to other things, when need be. But once they start crawling, you must always be on alert and make sure you have safety gates and to childproof cabinets, etc. Also, they're not always easy to see because they're so close to the ground. If you don't constantly have your eyes on them, you have to search for them. I also felt I needed to be very vigilant about the cleanliness of the floors because they're crawling on their hands and their hands and fingers would always go into their mouths. For this reason, I asked everyone who came into our house to please take their shoes off. I also needed to make sure the ground was clean and clear because they would put anything they found into their mouths.

I liked the walking stage much better. At least I could see them easier, now that they were higher up. Also, I didn't have to stress quite as much about the cleanliness of the floors, although I continued with the habit of asking people to take off their shoes when they came into the house because I read about what gets tracked in and it's disgusting. So now that I've gotten very used to them walking (and running, and jumping, etc.), I guess the next phase will be driving – YIKES!!

Their First Words

I was looking forward to when I would first be called "ma-ma". Then I knew I would really feel like a mom. And when that did eventually happen, it melted my heart and I loved it when each of my toddlers would say it to me. However, that was not the first word for either of them and it also wasn't "da-da". Zach's first word was "Bam!" and Alex's was "duck".

When Zach was a baby, we used to watch Emeril Lagasse's cooking show. If you know Emeril Lagasse, you know that he uses his signature "Bam!" in all his shows when he adds his special spices to what he cooks. Well, for some reason Zach really took to that and it became his first word, which David and I found very amusing. After that, we made sure to watch the show and have Zach watch it with us.

Alex's first word came from a book we used to read to the boys a lot. It was called "Mama Duck". It was about a baby duck who didn't listen to his mom when she told him to follow her and he got lost. He was very scared of all the unfamiliar things around him and was very relieved to finally find her. Well that book uses the word "duck" about 100 times or so, and that became Alex's first word. Also, we used to go to a nearby lake and feed the ducks with the boys. So, he always enjoyed pointing to all the ducks and saying "duck, duck" over and over again.

Preschool

Once Zach was eight months old, I went back to work. We were fortunate to live near his grandparents and they watched him twice a week, so I only had to take him to daycare three days a week. Once Alex was born, I tried to go back to work part-time, but they would only offer me a full-time position and after a lot of discussions, David and I decided I would not go back to work. However, I could see a benefit to having Zach and later Alex go to preschool to help with socialization and getting them ready for school. So, they were enrolled in preschool at the appropriate ages.

Unfortunately, I now know that the first preschool they went to turned into a less than desirable environment. There were staff changes that affected the atmosphere greatly. Eventually we found another preschool for Alex (Zach was already going into kindergarten). The new preschool was heads and shoulders above the previous one and I felt bad that I hadn't found this one in the first place. So a lesson to the wise, if you are looking for a preschool, go and shop around – a lot. Go to each one and talk to the director, teachers and look at the rooms. See if you can stop by at different times. When I was shopping around for our second preschool, I discovered that there are long waiting lists for some of them. So, this is good to know upfront so you can start looking as soon as possible.

The second preschool that Alex went to focused on socialization and getting them ready for kindergarten. In fact, they had a pre-kindergarten program that was very good. When both my boys entered kindergarten, they knew their letters, could write them all and knew their numbers up to 100. Alex even knew the numbers in Spanish up to ten – he's always liked learning and speaking Spanish.

I Hated Play-Doh

I know play-doh is a classic toy/plaything. And they say that it's easy to clean up. Just wait till it hardens, then simply pick it up. But the thing is, whenever my boys played with it, there was play-doh everywhere. There would be play-doh all over the floor, all over the table, under the table, on the table legs, on the seat of the chairs, then they would sit on it. There would be little squashed bits of play-doh on their clothes, then wherever they walked they would somehow spread play-doh around. I would then find it in the carpet, on the couches, in their bed, etc. And it's not so easy to clean up if it's squashed into your carpet or your sofa, even if it has dried. And it sometimes falls into small clumps that spread out in amazingly diverse areas, so you keep finding bright blue, red, yellow, green, orange, purple and all sorts of colors in each room of the house.

I started having the boys only play it outside on our patio, then our patio started getting stained with it. I would even spread newspapers under the table they were using. They would get up off the table and the newspapers would scrunch together or start blowing away and no matter how hard I tried, there would be little bits of play-doh squished into our patio. Then when they were finished, I would have to have them change their clothes right away so they didn't distribute play-doh all over the house from the bits that were inevitably squashed on their clothes. No thank you! I finally decided that preschool, pre-kindergarten and kindergarten were fine places for them to practice their sculpting skills. No more play-doh at home – I had had it. I know it must have been invented by a man!

Once They Start School

First Day of School

Getting ready for the first day of school was always an exciting time period. It was fun getting all the school supplies and having a bunch of brand new stuff. The boys especially enjoyed picking out their backpacks and lunchboxes. In the beginning, I went shopping with both of them and it was a bit chaotic making sure I had all the supplies listed on both their lists. As they got older, I decided to take them shopping one at a time. This seemed to make it more special also because they would get some one-on-one time with me while the other got alone time with David.

Then the next big surprise would be finding out who was going to be their teacher and who was in their class. Our school would make us wait until two days before school started. We all guessed they did this because they didn't want to deal with a lot of complaints. Sometimes we were thrilled, sometimes not.

One year in particular, I was worried because a few of Zach's friends were together in another class and Zach didn't seem to have anyone in his class that he knew real well. What I learned over that year, though, was that as the kids get older it doesn't matter as much if they're in the same class. They still play together at recess and lunch regardless. Also, he got to know a couple of new kids in his class that he might not have otherwise.

The first day is very exciting. The boys actually wake up on time, full of energy. They sometimes get down to the kitchen table before breakfast is actually ready. That hardly ever happens once the school year is in full swing. I always make them a special breakfast that I know they love and that has protein to keep them going throughout their energy-packed day. The boys are usually ready early and want to hurry up to get to school. It's funny – on the first day of the new year at our school there are always a lot of parents milling around. You never see as many dads as you do that first day. Once the bell rings, the kids line up and the teacher comes out and goes down the line saying hi to each child and their parents. The kids are always amazed that the teacher already knows them by name. Then the kids pile into the room and the parents are free! When the boys come home from school, they're always so excited and talk about how cool the day was. I love the first day! I always hope and try to find ways to keep that excitement or at least some of that enthusiasm going for as long as possible.

Stepping Out

For Zach's 9th birthday, we decided to get him a cell phone, which he had been desperately asking for. One of the reasons for this is that we decided he was old enough to walk home from school by himself. The cell phone made me feel safer about it. We live very close to his school – he doesn't even have to cross any streets. So we got him one of those pay-as-you-go plans and set some ground rules for its use. Everything went really well – he was responsible with his phone and if he was late coming home, I could get a hold of him to find out why. It really helped one day when he was able to call me to let me know he needed to stay after school to work on a project. Since we had such a positive experience with Zach, we decided to get a cell phone for Alex, too, for his 9th birthday. Then we let him walk home from school alone. He would walk to school with Zach, but they got out at different times, so they would each walk home alone. Again, Alex proved to be responsible and it worked well.

One Friday afternoon about two weeks before Christmas I was checking my e-mails. There was an e-mail from the school to all the parents. That morning a man had tried to offer a ride to a 9-year old girl from our school as she was walking to school. It was scary and shocking because we live in a very safe community. I know that's what people always say when something happens in their town, but we all really did feel safe here. (At the time this was written, Irvine had been the FBI's safest city with a population of over 100,000 people for five years in a row.) Later that evening, the story was mentioned on Los

Angeles TV news programs. I later learned that it happened at an intersection in our small neighborhood! I walk close to that intersection every school day. Zach walks near it every day on his way home! That shook me!! Then I got on the internet and found out that not only did this man offer this 9-year old girl (Zach's age) a ride to school, but he got out of his car and when she said "no", he tried to grab her! Now I was scared!

All of the parents were talking about this incident and many more parents, me included, started accompanying their children when they walked to or from school. We reiterated to our children the dangers of adults stopping them on the street and reminded them of safety rules. Eventually, the shock wore off, we all came back to school from Winter Break and things more or less went back to normal. I finally let Zach walk home without me again as long as he had his cell phone with him. I would wait in front of the house when it was time for him to be home and wait to see him walk around the corner. I wouldn't let him walk alone to his friend's house anymore, but we adjusted to either Alex and me walking with him or me driving him and dropping him off.

Then less than six months later, Zach's and Alex's school was locked-down one afternoon. I had been home and had noticed a helicopter circling our area. I turned on local news and looked on the internet to try to find out what was going on. Of course, I couldn't find any information. I was getting ready to leave to pick up the boys when the phone rang. It was an automated message from the school, saying that the school was locked-down because of police activity in the immediate area. They instructed us to pick our children up at the entrance to the front office. I quickly left, feeling very nervous and not knowing what was happening. When I got to the school, there was a swarm of parents near the front office. There were a number of police officers making sure every child had a parent present before they were released. There were police cars everywhere! I found out later that there had been an armed robbery in our little neighborhood (our neighborhood again!) They hadn't caught the suspect yet so they locked-down the school. Later that day the suspect was caught and a semi-automatic gun and ammunition were retrieved.

Both these incidents taught us that you can never completely let your guard down. Just when you exhale and feel secure about giving your children more freedom, things like this happen. However, you cannot let fear completely rule your life and you need to give your children age-appropriate independence so they can learn to successfully navigate through their world. This is just one of those acts of balance we parents have to make based on our individual situations.

I remember the first time we let one of our sons go to an amusement park without us. A friend of Zach's invited him to go to Legoland with his family. We've known this friend and his family for a couple of years. I said yes with no hesitation, knowing that he would be well taken care of and that he was old enough to be responsible and stay with the pack. However, as I got him ready to go, I did feel a certain unease/nervousness because he's going to be more than an hour away at an amusement park full of strangers. Sometimes your brain starts playing "what ifs," even though you really don't feel any of those things are likely to happen. I made sure he had a note in his pocket with my cell phone number and his friend's mom's cell phone number in case he got separated from them and reviewed that if he did get lost, go to someone who works there, not just some stranger. I then made sure the friend's mom had my home and cell phone numbers with her. Then I sent him off and told him to have a good time.

Friends

Helping your children develop and maintain friendships is a very important social skill for them to achieve. When my kids were toddlers, I would take them to the park and help them play nicely with other children – share, work together to build something in the sand, etc. I even tried meeting at a park regularly with a mom's group, but after a few tantrums, one vomiting incident and the time I put my diaper bag on the stroller handles and it tipped over with baby Alex screaming inside, it just got a little too embarrassing. I wondered why the other moms seemed more composed than me. What was it that I wasn't getting?

Then in preschool and kindergarten, you start setting up playdates. Sometimes we would meet at parks and the kids would play while the moms visited. Then we started doing more playdates at our houses. In the beginning, you learn not to have the visits last too long or the kids will get bored. Also, while they're this young, they don't play with any one thing for very long so they keep going from activity to another quickly and need your guidance. It starts to get exhausting because you're in constant motion. You start looking at the clock to see how close it is to pick-up time. Finally, as the children get older, playdates get easier. They start to be able to keep themselves occupied for longer periods of time and don't need your guidance as much. You eventually stop calling them playdates and just see if their friends can come over and hang out.

It's nice when you get a good rapport with the moms of your kids' friends and they reciprocate with having your kids over. There were always incidents when the friend's mom never or barely ever reciprocated. That would be irritating but I also realized that sometimes, there might be a good reason for that and I might just be more comfortable having the kids over at my house anyway. In any case, I realized that I was having friends over for the well-being of my sons so in the end, it didn't really matter if the other side reciprocated – I was still going to invite that friend over because my son liked him and wanted to spend time with him.

I noticed that before a new friend would come over, like when I knew his mom was going to come into the house to drop him off, I would clean the house and spruce myself up like company was coming over. This was kind of funny, but I wanted to make a good impression on the mom and make sure she felt comfortable having her son here. So in addition to straightening up, I would vacuum, clear off tables and counters (as much as possible), wipe down the bathroom sink and counter and re-fold the towels. I would brush my hair and make sure my makeup looked fresh. Then once we got to know each other better, I would relax more.

It works out great when the mom of your child's friend becomes your friend. I developed a few good friendships this way. It's fun for us and it's fun for the kids. Also, the kids end up spending more time together when you want to get together and visit with the other mom. I've even kept in touch with a couple of these mom-friends after the kids moved on.

Unfortunately, sometimes friendships sour and sometimes a good friend of your child starts acting mean. We had this experience and it was hard for David and me to watch our child go through it. Luckily, he communicated what was happening with us and we were able to talk it through with him. This particular friendship stayed strained for a couple of months until it finally ended. Our son had enough of this "friend" being mean and yelling at him and told him he was fed up. We were proud of our son for standing up for himself and learning how people should treat you, especially real friends. After this incident, we invited other boys over to build stronger friendships with some of his other acquaintances. Eventually, this boy apologized and they became friends again, but it taught all of us the importance of widening your social circle.

Another difficult situation we experienced mostly with our other son was when good friends would move away. Unfortunately, this happened to him more than a few times. Our school happened to have a relatively large number of families from other countries who were here on temporary job assignments. Our son had a few friends move away through the years, a couple of them best friends. We would try to keep in touch, but it was hard on our son to have to find other kids to hang out with after this. I just tried to help him develop other friendships and to widen his social circle.

Dick and Jane Moment

Jane had a crush on her flamboyant, gay hair stylist. She would let him cut my hair the way he wanted. So, he always gave me an ugly pageboy haircut (not the cute kind) that made me look like a little boy (hmm … I wonder why). Meanwhile, my dad was very frugal and would buy our jeans from Sears, where he worked. So I would walk around with stiff, boxy jeans from Sears in an ugly pageboy haircut. Frankly, I looked rather butch. I definitely wasn't one of the "cool" kids at school.

Homework

I was actually looking forward to the day when Zach and Alex would have homework when they were younger (what was I thinking?) I thought it would be fun to help them with it and supervise them as they were completing it. It was fun in the beginning because it wasn't very difficult for them and they were excited about it because it made them feel like "big kids". However, the novelty wore off rather quickly. They started complaining about it and taking longer to complete it because they would get distracted easily. Then as they moved up in elementary school, it got harder and they needed more help from me, and sometimes David, especially when they were working on reports and projects. School theoretically teaches them how to compile information, outline it, then write and rewrite it, but when they're first learning these skills, they need your help with most of this.

I talked to other moms to gauge if they were having the same experience and basically, yes. We all had varying degrees of involvement and it would differ according to the report or project, but yes, we were helping them sift, sort, write, etc. The one thing that drove me crazy is what I call "busy work". When they have to build a model or make a visual aid, this can be very much "busy work" that the parents really need to help them with. This doesn't actually help the child learn the material, it's just an added factor. It may seem like it would be a fun project that uses their imaginations, but this is really just true theoretically. Because in real life, you have a tight timeline. You're using most of your time on the meat and bones of the project and having to deal with something to build or create on top of that just adds stress.

Homework did at times become an issue that I would end up arguing and nagging my children over. Then after talking to teachers I realized, I'll just back off. I'll tell them it's their homework and their responsibility to complete it to the best of their ability. I'm there to assist them if they need it or help guide them, but it's basically their responsibility. This way, if it's not completed or they obviously did a shabby job just to quickly get it over with, they have to deal with the consequences. My job was to make sure they had a reasonably comfortable place to do their homework and to make sure they weren't watching TV, using the computer, etc. before homework was completed. I also checked their homework, not to correct any mistakes, but to make sure they were doing their best work. However, I couldn't always stick to this hands-off approach. When one of them got a "D" on his progress report, I started monitoring his homework again because I just couldn't stand by when his grades slipped that much.

Homework became a whole other issue in middle school. The kids were sometimes spending three or four hours a day on homework. I started discussing this with other moms to see if they were having the same experience and many of them did. Also, the kids had homework every weekend. They were given math homework Monday through Friday, so it was a given that they would have math homework every weekend, but they were getting homework in other subjects, too. During Labor Day weekend, our middle school son was working on homework all throughout the 3-day holiday. We had thought about taking a trip to Lake Arrowhead and it turned out to be a good thing that we didn't plan that trip, because our son would have spent most of his time up there doing homework and that would have ruined it for us.

Finally, some of us moms asked that the subject of homework be addressed at an upcoming PTA meeting. We had been told at the beginning of the year that there was a district-wide revised homework policy. We thought that meant that the amount of homework would be reduced. Now we wanted clarification about what this revised policy really meant. I spoke during the PTA meeting about the amount of time the children were spending on homework, the fact that they have homework every weekend and during breaks, and how, as a family, we want to spend time together during breaks and weekends. I also mentioned our concern that this amount of homework was beginning to burn out the kids and cause them to lose their love of learning.

Long story short, I think it made some difference, but maybe not a huge impact. They will continue to get math homework every weekend because the math teachers feel that they need the practice to learn math effectively. However, it does seem that the teachers are trying harder to give them time in class to start on their homework so there's less of a workload once they get home.

I have to add in here that while we were having struggles with homework with our middle school child, our other son would come home and promptly take his homework out of his backpack and complete it. He didn't even take a break when he first got home, he just wanted to get it finished. At the same time, he was doing good work and not just plowing through it, as evidenced by his grades. We were very proud of his being such a successful self-starter.

Helping Them Do Their Best on Tests

Nobody likes taking tests, but we found some strategies that were useful to help our kids do their best for tests and not stress out too much. Here are some things that worked for our family:

- Don't make tests seem like a huge affair. This just sets up a state of anxiety in which the person worries how they will do that day. Highlight the fact that a test is just a way of finding out how much they've learned about a subject. Therefore, if they have been studying, doing their homework and paying attention in class, they should do well. We always told our kids to just do their best. What wasn't acceptable was to be lazy and not study or try hard enough.

- Try to get enough sleep the night before. This is crucial because a sleepy brain is not a sharp one. However, this was difficult for us because our children were night-owls. We would try to get them to go to sleep in a timely manner by not letting them use any electronics after dinner, so they wouldn't get stimulated by them. We also tried to keep things as quiet as possible, so everyone would naturally wind down.

- Study right before going to sleep. There are two reasons for this. First, it can get the child sleepy, as it's a fairly boring activity. Second, there have been studies showing that if you study something before you go to sleep, your brain will process it during sleep and help you to remember it.

- Have a balanced, healthy breakfast with some protein. You need to feed your child's brain to make sure it's operating at peak performance. It's important to feed your child some protein before a test to stabilize blood sugar levels for a long period of time. However, make sure you're giving them a healthy breakfast and not just a big, fat-laden one, which can actually make them feel sluggish. You want your child to feel peppy, awake and sharp.

These strategies helped our sons do well on their tests. You can't take their tests for them, but you can give them the best tools possible to help them succeed.

Classroom/School Volunteering

I volunteered for both my sons' classes every year from kindergarten to 6th grade, when the teachers didn't need parent volunteers in the classrooms anymore. I loved being able to see how the classrooms really operated and getting to know the teachers and the other classmates better. I also loved how happy my boys were to see me in their classes. They were always very proud to have me there.

I enjoyed going on their field trips also. They were enjoyable and enlightening and I liked seeing how all the kids interacted together and getting more of a glimpse of my child's day. One field trip I especially liked surprised me because I didn't expect that much from it. We went to a park that had old buildings from the 1890's. It was very educational and the buildings and items within were refurbished so you really got the feel of what it must have been like to live in that time period. The docent who led us through the buildings and surrounding areas was very patient and explained information in a fun way. The children got to practice doing laundry the way they used to, by scrubbing cloth on a washboard, wringing it dry, then hanging it on a line. They got to take turns crushing corn to make cornmeal. They got to be students in an old schoolhouse and get the feeling of what it would be like to have a teacher teach different grade levels (1st through 8th).

One year I decided to become room mom for both of my sons' classes. I did this because I had always volunteered in their classes each week and had come to most of their room parties and field trips, so I'd always done a lot of what a room mom does except plan the parties and manage the money. Also, Zach was in 5th grade and I had been told by other moms that you don't volunteer in their classes once they start 6th grade. So, I figured I only had one more year to do this for Zach and if I did it for him, I should also do it for Alex. Therefore, I decided to just take the plunge and try it.

Let me digress for a moment and explain that when I signed up to be room mom in both classes, I meant to be one of three or four room moms. However, I somehow became HEAD room mom in both classes, which surprised and kind of worried me because I had never been room mom before. For some reason, the teacher from Zach's class signed me up as the head room mom and no other moms signed up for Alex's class. I was scared when I found out I was the only room mom in the 3rd grade class. The teacher asked two other moms if they would help me and they agreed. They ended up helping a lot and I became friends with one who I hadn't previously known and became better friends with the other one. So, I ended up being in charge of all the money for the two classes, sending letters to parents, planning parties, figuring out teacher gifts, etc.

It ended up turning out well but there were some whirlwind times, especially at the end of the year. During the last two months of school, I was planning and organizing Alex's teacher's birthday celebration, a pool party, three lunches (two on the last day of school), Zach's teacher's baby shower and also putting together scrapbooks for each teacher as an end-of-the-year gift and being head of a committee for a special day called American Heritage Day (whew!). One of the other moms said I was going to get sick if I wasn't careful!

During this time I had to send multiple letters to parents in both classes, collect money, collect scrapbook pages from the kids, get kids to sign cards without the teachers knowing, buy gifts, cards, food items, etc. The amount of details was staggering! I woke up a number of nights with details swimming around in my head because I was so afraid of forgetting something. I had a long to-do list and then would break it down day by day so I wouldn't forget important deadlines. Somehow it all came together and it was all successful. I had good help from several moms, which made it manageable and more pleasant.

OK - so now would I do it again?

If I had the same choice at the beginning of the year, I would do it again. I formed some new relationships and built some closer relationships. I got to know the teachers much more personally than I would have and I was fortunate that I really liked the teachers! My sons enjoyed that I was so involved and enjoyed seeing me in their classes so much, although I do know they have no idea how much behind-the-scenes work I was doing. The best part of this experience was that the boys did get a sense of pride having me be "head" room mom in each of their classes. I also enjoyed the sense of accomplishment from actually achieving success in this endeavor. I haven't worked officially for almost a decade and this taught me that I still have marketable skills, namely managing, organizing, planning and negotiating. It felt good to use these skills again and know that they haven't atrophied.

Will I be room mom again in either of their classes? I won't say never, but I've done it, it was successful and why push fate? The down-side was that family issues came up during the year that I wasn't able to put my full attention to or effort into. And that sometimes made me sad. I also realized that I did this mostly for my sons and if I neglected other issues that affect them because I'm caught up in details and busywork, then I'm not really doing what I set out to do - I'm not reaching my real goal - to stand beside them with support and guidance. So I've continued to volunteer in their classes, go to parties and field trips, but I don't sign up to be a room mom now.

Relationships with Their Teachers and Coaches

As your children progress through their school years, you will find teachers that you think are wonderful and teachers that you wonder about. For some of their teachers you think, "well they just have to get through one year". Other teachers you think, "can you please decide to move to the next grade level so they can have you again?" I have experienced both with my sons.

Whichever type the teacher is I have tried to get to know them better through volunteering in their classes and always keeping the lines of communication open. I would also try to help out during parties, chaperone field trips and buy supplies she/he might need in the classroom. This shows you're interested and involved, and like any relationship, teachers tend to respond to that. When I've had questions or concerns, I've asked to set up a meeting with them at their convenience. They like knowing that a parent is involved, that you want to work as a team and that you value their input and their professional expertise during the day.

It's also great to get to know them a bit more personally. I would talk to them about their day-to-day lives, their families, their interests. The more we could relate to each other, the better your bond and that only helps your child. I'm not saying this to be insincere, I'm just saying that it can be nice to get to know them beyond school and sometimes you find you have some common interests.

With regard to coaches, I have mostly greatly appreciated their input and time. Most of the coaches in the sports our sons played were volunteer dads. They took time out of their schedules to do this and they really made an effort to help the kids and encourage them. I welcomed their input and influence on my sons. I made sure to tell my sons to pay attention to them and always act respectfully towards them. David and I would get to know our sons' coaches through watching their practices and games and chatting with them. There were some fantastic coaches who, like fantastic teachers, made an extremely favorable impression on our sons and taught them in a way that we never could. Additionally, your kids don't always listen to you the way the will to someone else – that's just the way it is.

Stepping In or Butting Out

It's hard to watch your child go through a difficult situation or learn a hard lesson. We always want to protect them and make things better. But we realize we can't do this forever and that our goal is to raise self-sufficient, productive, happy adults. Teaching your children how to handle adversity and disappointments and that they will survive, learn and ultimately thrive builds resilience. Sometimes they need to just learn that things don't always go their way and to put it into perspective – will this really matter five years from now?

In line with this, there are times during your children's lives when you have to decide whether your best action as a parent is to step in for your child or butt out and let him/her figure it out. If we step in too much for them, they don't learn to be their own champion. However, we can't always completely butt out because sometimes they need our support in the face of situations they haven't learned to handle yet or that need more persuasion or pressure on our part.

It's good to sometimes help them to brainstorm potential solutions because it's best if they come up with it on their own. It's fine if your guidance helps them, but sometimes they can come up with a better solution than us because they're living in the situation and can see it more clearly. As my sons got older, I learned to encourage them to brainstorm the best way to handle a situation and then try that. If it didn't work, then David and/or I would get involved, especially if it had to do with school. This strategy strengthened their confidence while letting them know that we would always be there to support them if need be.

For example, there were numerous instances at school where David and I would need to decide when and if we needed to get involved. Some were minor issues, like one of the boys forgetting their homework, a project, a book, a binder, etc. When they were younger and it was something important, like a project they had been working on or a binder with information I knew they would need, I would try to take it to them at school. However, I learned quickly that the teachers didn't like this and I also realized that the boys needed to learn responsibility and that sometimes it meant them getting in trouble or taking a lower grade for not turning in work on time.

Later, other more important issues would come up like discipline issues, bullying or falling grades. David and I did need to get involved with some of these issues because we needed to work directly with the teachers and the school to figure out exactly what was going on and how to resolve it. As the boys got even older, however, we pulled back more and encouraged them to go to their teachers directly or work with a specific student or situation themselves. Then if a resolution was not happening, David and/or I would get involved. It continues to be a push-pull situation, but we have been proud of how the boys have learned to deal with situations and stand up for themselves.

It Takes a Village

It really does help to have a network of support around you while raising children whether it's family, friends, neighbors, community members or some combination of all these. Having a number of loving, supporting people in their lives helps make children feel valued and safe. It also gives them a broader view of the world.

A very important element of this village is school. I was always very involved in Zach's and Alex's school, volunteering in their classrooms, being a member of PTA, chaperoning field-trips, being one of the class moms, etc. I loved being able to be so involved at their school. This gave me a hands-on view of what was going on in their classrooms and it gave me the opportunity to get to know their teachers and classmates so much better. Also, the boys loved seeing me come to their classrooms to help. Their smiles were the most gratifying aspect of it. I also got to know other parents, the principal and the staff better.

Through the years we were very fortunate to have a very strong network of support through our family. Grandparents, aunts, uncles, etc. were always around and very involved in our children's lives. Whenever we had an emergency (there were quite a few), we had a number of family members we could call on for help.

One such emergency occurred when Alex was just about 3 months old. David had gone on a weeklong business trip to New York. That evening a friend of mine from work came over and had dinner with the boys and me. It happened to be the night before trash pickup in our neighborhood and we would usually put the trash out in the evening. As I was taking the trash bin out to our curb, my sandal slipped off my foot and I stumbled on the sandal and twisted my ankle as I tried to keep from falling. It became apparent fairly quickly that something was terribly wrong, as I realized I couldn't put any weight on my foot. My friend had to drive the boys and me to the emergency room and then stay with them in the waiting area while they took care of me, bless her. Mind you, she was not a parent herself and was watching a 3-month old and 1 ½ year old. Well, I ended up having a broken foot.

For the rest of the week, I needed someone to spend the night with us every night because Alex still had to eat in the middle of the night and I was on crutches and couldn't get him out of the crib. Different family members rallied around with their support and took turns staying with the boys and me. I didn't tell David what happened because he was all the way in New York and I wasn't sure he could even come home early, so then he would just be there worrying and it would be affecting his work. Also, because of family members' being so gracious, the boys and I were being taken care of and we were fine. David sure was surprised when he got home and saw Uncle Brian holding Alex and wondered, "why is he here?" Then he saw me standing behind Uncle Brian with crutches!

Ready, Set, GO

When it comes to introducing your children to activities, you want to expose them to as much as possible to figure out what they will like and be good at. You always hear about prodigies who started when they were 4 or 5 years old. So, you feel a pressure to expose them to as much as possible as soon as possible, lest they fall behind everyone else.

Activities we've tried with Zach and Alex are soccer, basketball, baseball, swimming, Tae Kwon Do, art, guitar, tennis, skiing, snowboarding, ice skating, roller skating/blading, skateboarding, foreign language, Cub Scouts, etc. There are still a lot of activities we want to introduce them to, but you run out of time and thankfully, they start knowing better what their interests are. There was a season when each son was involved in three different activities. That was crazy but they were very interested in all of them. That season there was something going on six days a week, with practices, lessons or games overlapping on most of these days. I was running around, the boys were running around and although it was fun (for them), it got too stressful. We limited the activities to two per son and they just had to pick and choose.

When Zach went into fourth grade, the homework got harder and more time-consuming. He also wanted more time to just play and hang out with friends. Therefore, he started just picking one activity per season. Also, as the children get older, they have more practices per week for each sport. We learned to stop running around like the proverbial chicken with its head cut off and to prioritize what they really wanted to focus on. We became calmer and they actually got more time to just hang out, which is really important to their development.

Many moms I've talked to have dealt with juggling activities and we eventually figure out a balance that works for us and our families. It's always a work in progress, though, as new seasons start and old ones end. We just all hope we gave our children the opportunities they needed to excel in their chosen pursuits.

The other day I drove by the pool where they used to have practices when they were on the Novaquatics swim team, an Irvine swim club where Olympic medalists such as Aaron Piersol, Amanda Beard, Jason Lezak and others trained. I saw a bunch of tents set up and saw that the parking lot was full. I had to smile, realizing that if they were still on the swim team, our weekend would have been full, with a meet on both days. I liked it enough while they were doing it but it was nice to realize that we had a mostly open weekend instead, where we could just choose to do what we wanted.

During summer vacation, I usually sign the boys up for some sort of half-day camps. I usually just sign them up for a week or two because they generally only have about five weeks off since they go to a year-round school. I sign them up for enough time, so they don't get completely bored and they get to decide which activities they want to do.

In the summer of 2009, however, I decided not to sign them up for any camps to save money. I was worried that they would get bored and I would be tearing my hair out. But what actually happened is that we all enjoyed the rest and not having to run around on a timetable. The boys slept in each morning and I had time to get on my exercise bike after David left for work and before the boys woke up. Then we had lazy mornings where I could decide what to make for breakfast based solely on what we all wanted because I had the time. They kept themselves occupied by playing games that they made up together and we had their friends over, went to the pool a lot, went to the library, etc. It was a very unhurried and relaxing summer and I feel it really gave them the respite they and I needed to start another school year.

Daily Routines

When your children are babies, you don't really have a routine at first. You crave a routine but at first you just have to feed your baby every couple of hours and change diapers in between. Your days and nights are filled with feeding, changing, trying to squeeze in as much sleep as possible and doing whatever chores and hygiene tasks you can in between. Finally as your baby gets older, you are able to fall into a fairly predictable routine. When my children were babies and toddlers my routine was pretty much as follows:

> They would wake up around 6 a.m., slip into bed with me and we would watch Sesame Street. We would cuddle and wake up slowly – it was a very sweet way to begin the day. Then we would have breakfast and slowly begin our day.
>
> For a while, they would need a morning nap and an afternoon nap, so the day was always planned accordingly. I found out through trial and error that you really didn't want to keep a sleepy baby away from his nap for too long or you would pay for it. So, during that time I couldn't get much done away from the house in the morning – maybe a quick errand. The morning nap would last for about an hour. Then I would have a few hours before the afternoon nap to take them to a park or run some errands and feed them lunch.

The afternoon nap would last about two hours and it was a really sweet time of day. It was early-mid afternoon and they were all sleepy and the house would be nice and quiet. I used this time to get caught up on chores and sometimes I snuck in a 20-30 minute nap also. After the nap we could do whatever until dinner.

After dinner, there were about two hours at most until bedtime so that time would be used up by bathtime, storytime and lullaby's. Then I would have about two hours or so to myself and to spend with my husband. I would actually get some exercise done in the evenings. As they got older, they dropped their morning nap, which was easier because I had a longer period where I could be out of the house getting things done or just having fun with them.

Once the boys were in school the routine changed because of course, I had more alone time during the day to get things done. The mornings became more hectic because they had to be fed and ready to go to school by a certain time. And the afternoons became busier because they had homework and after-school activities.

Then there was dinnertime and getting things ready before bedtime. They went to bed later, stayed awake longer after being put to bed, and the time between them falling asleep and me getting ready for bed diminished. Therefore, I needed to run all my errands and get most of my chores done while they were in school. In fact, afternoons and evenings became very hectic during this time because they would both be involved in different sports and I would be running them around and staying to watch practices when they were too young to be dropped off. There wasn't always enough time to get homework done before practices, so they would have to finish it while I was making dinner. I was routinely getting interrupted because they needed help with homework. So, dinner would inevitably take awhile to prepare.

Then after dinner, they would need to take showers and finish any left-over homework. They would then read to David and me, one parent per child and we would alternate, until they got old enough to read on their own. When they were reading to us, we would try to read to them afterwards if there was enough time. Eventually, though, that got dropped as they got old enough to read quietly to themselves and their bedtime got pushed back. Then it became a struggle to get them to brush their teeth, get ready for bed and then to eventually stop reading and go to bed. Once lights were out, it would take them a while to simmer down enough to fall asleep. By that time, David and I were falling asleep also.

The Morning Rush

We've got our mornings down pretty well now. I get up half an hour before the kids to get myself ready. Then I go wake each boy up. I actually love this part of the day because I get to wake them up with a couple of kisses (sorry to embarrass you guys). I'm usually not allowed to kiss them, but in the morning they're so tired that their resistance is down, and I darn well take advantage of that! Then I go downstairs to make their breakfast

Most times it takes them about half an hour to actually get downstairs. All they have to do is dress themselves, but it takes half an hour for them to drag themselves out of bed to do this. I guess they need the time to slowly acclimate themselves to the idea of actually becoming conscious and this works well for us because it gives me time to make sure breakfast is ready by the time they get downstairs. Then they have to eat fairly quickly so they have time to get upstairs and brush their teeth, then pack any odds and ends before they walk out the door. They have about 25 minutes to do all this if it takes them 30 minutes to get downstairs.

I have repeatedly asked them to please pack their backpacks at night or in the afternoon once they have completed their homework so we're not scrambling around at the last minute looking for books or loose papers. However, they tend to fail to do this. As a result, they both have left books or homework accidentally at home. I used to try to get it to them when I realized this, but now they're old enough to learn the consequences of not obeying me. If they get a lower mark because their homework is turned in late, so be it – they have to learn.

I've also stopped myself from yelling at them to hurry up and get out the door or they'll be late. I know that this is a lesson they also have to learn. If they're late, they have to go to the office and get a pass before they can go into their classroom. This way they learn that they will have to pay and feel embarrassed if they dawdle too much. I have to remember that it doesn't really affect me – it's ultimately their decision.

One rule I learned early on is that there is absolutely no TV viewing in the morning. If the TV came on, it was almost impossible to keep the boys focused on getting ready and to get them out the door. They got used to this rule rather quickly and we don't have a problem with it anymore. I also found out that the morning runs smoother if I wait to eat until the boys have left and I've walked the dog. That way I can focus on everything getting done to get the boys successfully out the door. When they were younger, I would walk them to school. Then as they got older, I would walk them to an adjoining gate to the school's field with our dog. Now, they just walk to school alone and I make sure to wish them a good day before they leave. I don't get to kiss them or hug them or anything, but I guess I can wait till the next morning.

Dick and Jane Moment

We had a huge Saint Bernard dog named Timothy. Sometimes in the morning when we were rushing to get to school and were late, as usual, Timothy would bite the tires on our car as my mom was trying to back up and drive away because he didn't want us to leave. Jane would be screaming frantically while he was lunging at our tires and my brothers and I were afraid he would get hurt. He was so strong that he actually made our tires flat a couple of times.

The Evening Countdown

Unfortunately, there's usually so much to get done in the evening. It's hard to get everyone to slow down enough to really get ready for sleeping. The boys are usually finishing up homework or watching TV while I'm making dinner. We try to always eat together as a family but sometimes David gets home late from work and the boys are starving.

It drives me crazy when dinner is about 15 min. away and the boys keep trying to raid the cupboard and refrigerator. It's not as if they haven't been eating all afternoon long. When they get home from school I try to have a variety of fruits available that they can choose from and sometimes cut up carrots or celery. But they always want something unhealthy, too, like ice cream, chips or cookies. Many times, I'll let them have one unhealthy thing as long as everything else they're snacking on is healthy. I also try to make them more substantial snacks like Chinese dumplings or big, soft pretzels. I offer them nuts and hard-boiled eggs to try to give them more sustenance, too. No matter what I do, though, they always seem to be starving 15 min. before dinner.

After dinner, they need to take their showers and get ready for bed. Then it's time for some reading. Through the years it's changed from us reading to them, to them reading aloud to us to practice their reading, to them reading by themselves alone. After they started reading to themselves, David and I would still sometimes try to read to them from chapter books if they got to bed early enough.

One of the series we had fun reading to them was *Harry Potter*. David and I really liked these stories as well and after finishing a book, we would rent the movie. However, this only worked with the first two books of the series. It was taking a really long time trying to get through the third book and Alex wanted to hurry up and see the movie because a number of his friends had already seen it and really liked it. One of the problems we encountered with the third book was that the chapters were so long. They would get disinterested and bored or we would get so tired during the middle of a chapter that I would finally just have to stop. We didn't always have enough time for this reading, so if it was a couple of days later, it was hard to pick up where we left off. I would inevitably have to go back to remind us of what was going on, then we wouldn't finish the chapter that evening, and that pattern kept repeating. It just started getting too frustrating. So, I finally gave in and rented the movie and once the boys had seen the movie, they were no longer interested in reading the book. I tried to explain that we would all understand the story better if we read the book since it has so much more detail than the movie, but that wasn't motivating enough for them.

Finally, they got to the age where they got their own rooms. We tried to keep reading to them by taking turns on which room we would read in and the other boy would sit in his brother's room while we were reading, but eventually, the boys ended up reading to themselves and this worked out well because they were reading different books. We were just happy that they were keeping up this reading habit and they found a few other series they liked, so they found reading before bed enjoyable and it did relax them and help them get ready to fall asleep.

Whew! Thank God It's Monday!

Bet you thought you'd never say that before children. But sometimes weekends are filled with so many activities, that they are more exhausting and stressful than the rest of the week. When they get filled with different sports games, especially those that start early in the morning, and add in a birthday party, then maybe a family event and a get-together at your house that you have to shop, cook and clean for. During all of this, you're supposed to have fun and enjoy it all! And you're really, really trying to, but you feel so stressed and you're afraid you're going to forget something.

After a particularly active and stressful weekend, I actually wrote the following article which I was going to send to a local newspaper, which highlighted favorite weekends of different celebrities. I wanted to show the actual weekend of an everyday parent. Enjoy!

Start Winding Down

On Friday afternoon my two sons each have a friend over. For 2 ½ hours, there are four boys between the ages of seven and ten running up and down the stairs, fighting over who gets to use the computer, fighting over who gets to use the Wii and which game to play, looking for Star Wars Clone Wars guns, running outside and back inside numerous times while forgetting to take off their shoes and tracking in slurry seal all over our newly cleaned off-white carpets.

When the friends' mothers mercifully come to pick up their sons, I remind Zach that he has to change into his basketball uniform. When it's 15 minutes until his game starts and after copious amounts of yelling and taking privileges away, he saunters down the stairs and informs me he's hungry.

After watching the game (104 vs. 6), I decide which fast-food joint to drive through while consoling my son about the fact that the other team was a team of giants and the ref really wasn't making fair calls anyway. After the boys load up on cheeseburgers, fries, apple dippers and shakes and my husband and I microwave leftovers from three days ago, the boys argue over which show to watch on TV and I plop a bowl of popcorn in front of them. Then I grab a glass of wine and a magazine and sit on the sofa. I wake up at midnight to find my husband sprawled on the other sofa and the boys still watching TV and asking for more popcorn.

Ready, Set, Go

Saturday morning, I wake up to beep, beep, beeping as I realize I automatically set the alarm last night. It's now 6:30 in the morning. I put my head back on the pillow as I realize I have another hour to sleep. My husband hasn't stirred. As I lay awake during the whole hour, I think about the things to do this weekend, what I need to buy at the grocery store today, what meals I will make all week, I need to remember to make a doctor's appointment for Alex, I still haven't bought the gift for the birthday party Alex will go to tomorrow, I forgot the clothes in the washer last night, the credit card bill is due in two days – if I drive to the post office to mail it today, will it get there in time?

When I get up, I remember that Alex's soccer uniform hasn't been washed and is all rumpled at the bottom of the laundry basket. As

I throw the clothes from the washer into the dryer and throw the uniform into the washer, I calculate I will have just enough time for the uniform to dry before we run out the door to his game. I wake the boys up, I wake my husband up and the rush is on to get everyone fed, dressed and teeth brushed while keeping the boys from becoming comatose in front of the TV. As Alex is putting his soccer socks on he says “mom, why do my socks feel wet?” “Don’t worry hon, they’ll dry out before the game” (I hope).

While we watch Alex’s game, I remember that I’m supposed to bring the snack for Zach’s game, which starts in an hour. I rush to the store to pick up chips, fruit roll-ups and juice and make it back to Alex’s game to find out I just missed the first goal he’s ever made. “Mom, where were you?” – ouch!

After Zach’s game, I go grocery shopping, stop at the dry cleaners, drop off bills at the post office, stop at the pharmacy, get gas and deposit money at the bank’s ATM to cover the bills I just mailed. It’s dinner time by the time I get home and Alex has a basketball game in an hour. I make the boys hot dogs, have some cereal, then throw in another load of laundry before we head out the door.

When we get back from the game, the boys argue over which show to watch on TV. I’m too tired to make popcorn so they each eat a bag of chips. I get myself a glass of wine and a magazine and sit on the sofa. At midnight I wake up to see the boys eating another bag of chips, while there are four empty chip bags surrounding them, and my husband is sprawled on the other sofa.

A Relaxing Sunday

Ahh, Sunday at last! I finally get to sleep in. The cat comes in our room at 5:50 and jumps on the bed, then jumps on the windowsill, then starts scratching the side of our bed "Zoey, cut it out!", then goes into the bathroom and finds an errant marble on the floor and starts chasing it around, bouncing it off the walls.

After about ½ an hour, I decide to just get up. My husband hasn't stirred. I go out to get the newspaper and start going through it. Once I get comfortable, the boys wake up and start yelling that they're hungry. I make them pancakes from scratch and try to make a clever shape out of them. "What is that?" "I know – it's a cat's head." "No, you guys, it's a birthday present with ribbon – Alex's birthday is coming up – can't you see?" "Uh yeah, mom, whatever."

Then I remember that I still haven't gotten the gift for the birthday party Alex will be going to in an hour. I get dressed and rush to Target to find Bakugan, or Gormiti, or whatever was popular with boys his age at the time. When I get home, I realize I forgot to get a card so I put a green piece of paper in front of Alex and tell him to make one – "it's more special that way – really."

When Alex and I get to Boomers, a family entertainment center that's a very popular place for birthday parties, we're searching for anyone we can recognize in a sea of screaming, hyped-up, sugar-loaded, token-wielding children. After a day of miniature golf, laser tag, bumper boats, race cars and the kiddy-casino - I mean the arcade - I'm looking forward to a relaxing Sunday evening.

When I get home, Zach informs me that he has a report due tomorrow on Chumash Indians and he can't get all his information on the internet. When we get to the library 15 minutes before it closes, a sympathetic librarian leads us to a book on Californian Indians. We gratefully rush home. After three hours of finding out as much as we can about the Chumash and me lecturing Zach that he needs to write the report himself because it's his report, not mine, I argue with the boys about taking showers, brushing teeth and going to bed.

When I hit the pillow, I'm out. Then I wake up at 3:07 and hear a drip, drip, dripping. I remember that I need to call the plumber about the leak in the shower faucet that keeps getting worse, I need to collect money and get a gift for Zach's coach, I need to buy party favors for Alex's upcoming birthday party, I need to bake cookies for the PTA bake sale on Tuesday, I've got to buy baseball cleats before the season starts, I need to start working on our taxes, I need to fill out and turn in a field trip permission slip and I forgot about another load of laundry in the washer. I drift off to sleep somewhere around 6 (I stop looking at the clock at 5:37). The alarm goes off at 6:30. My husband hasn't stirred. Another ordinary weekend.

Special Times

Holidays

Holidays were always very fun and festive times, though very busy. One thing I loved was the pictures you take during holidays and how you can really see how your children change each year (and how we do, too, although that's not so fun). Here are some of my memories from various holidays.

New Year's Eve

Most of the time we would go to one of the aunt's houses and eat a bunch of appetizers and drink champagne (sparkling cider for the boys). We would watch New York welcome the new year, which was 9 p.m. for us. We would have poppers and the boys would set them off to celebrate. Then we would go home because I don't like to be on the road too late on New Year's Eve. When the boys were young, we would put them to bed when we got home and David and I would try to stay awake until midnight to usher in the real new year. Now that they're older, they have no problem staying up until midnight (unfortunately) and we'll all stay up and celebrate. Then we try to get them calmed down and into bed. We usually end up falling asleep before they do.

Easter

We would always start the morning with the boys looking for their Easter baskets, which the Easter Bunny had hidden. Then the boys' grandparents would come over for breakfast and afterwards, the boys would have an egg hunt. Then later in the afternoon, we would get together with other family members. We used to go to a nice restaurant by a lake until the 2008 recession. Then everyone needed to watch their money, so we would host an early potluck dinner. Eventually a couple of aunts hosted a brunch at their place. We've kept up this tradition as the boys have gotten older even though, of course, they no longer believe in the Easter Bunny – it's still fun for us to pretend.

4th of July

Our city hosts a parade every 4th of July morning. They close a certain stretch of road near a lake and anyone who wants to can walk the route and be part of the parade. People wear red, white and blue and decorate bikes, razors, golf carts and various types of floats that they make. We would watch the parade, then go to breakfast at a nearby restaurant. Then we would do whatever we felt like during the day and have a BBQ in the evening, usually with a couple of aunts. Then there was a place nearby which would have a free firework show. We would watch at a nearby school where they actually allowed people to set off their own fireworks. So, we would have a lot of fun doing this until the show began and it was a great way to use up the waiting time.

Halloween

When the boys were very young, it was easy to get their Halloween costumes. I would just pick out whatever looked cute and they wouldn't complain. Then as they got older and started to get into certain themed toys, they wanted to pick out their own costumes like Teenage Mutant Ninja Turtles, Power Rangers, Star Wars characters, etc. I'm not much of a crafty person so I always went to party stores or those Halloween stores that crop up the couple months before Halloween. I would try to stick to a budget and the boys were really good about it. I didn't like the idea of them getting costumes that got too gory and they were good about that too. As they got even older, their costumes became less elaborate because it wasn't "cool" anymore to really be dressed in a costume. They would either try to find something to throw together that would be funny, clever or just stick a mask on.

There was a certain neighborhood we always drove to for trick-or-treating. We would usually hit our neighborhood for about a ½ hour, then drive to this other neighborhood. We found this neighborhood when we first moved to our city. One of our neighbors told us how cool it was and it was across the street from our tract of homes. It was such a scene!! The houses had elaborate decorations and one house would be decorated like an intricate haunted house each year. There were always so many kids, it was hard walking on the sidewalks!! Many of the people just set up chairs and tables in front of their garages to hand out candy to the swarms of kids. Some of the houses gave out full-sized candy bars, although that decreased quite a bit after the recession. Anyway, after about an hour of trick-or-treating, each son had a loaded pillowcase full of way too much candy. Eventually, that candy would go to a local food bank through their school, so at least the boys didn't eat it all. It was always fun to have their friends join us for trick-or-treating and fun to see their reactions when we get to that neighborhood.

Christmas

Of course, this was the biggest holiday of the year for us. Depending on what day Christmas Eve fell, some years we would go to the boys' grandparent's house and then to their aunts' house in the same afternoon and evening. When they were very young, this would be very chaotic and exhausting. There would be incredible amounts of packing and unpacking – diaper bag, high chair, toys to keep them busy, blankets, pacifiers, bottles, baby food, pajamas to change them into, let alone presents we were bringing and food and beverages for the parties. And God forbid you forgot anything. And this packing/unpacking would happen three different times with different items and we were trying to keep track of everything. Thankfully, this got simplified as they got older!

Then David and I would have to wait until the boys went to sleep to lay the presents out in the living room. As they got older, they took longer to fall asleep. David and I would be exhausted and we had to stay awake somehow. One Christmas Eve, Alex was still awake at midnight and he started crying because he thought Santa was going to pass over the house. We had always told the boys that Santa would only come after they were asleep. We felt so bad for Alex! We assured him that Santa would come in the early morning hours.

In the morning the boys would wake up hours before normal, of course, and full of energy! David and I would peel ourselves out of bed and stumble downstairs. Then mayhem followed. With wrapping paper and ribbon and bows flying, all the presents would be opened. When it was finished, it looked like a tornado had stormed across our living room. There were usually parts to put together, which David would do with the boys and they would play until it was time to go to another aunt's house for an early Christmas dinner. By the end of the evening, David and I felt like we were hit by trucks, but it was always a fun day and the boys were happy.

Dick and Jane Moment

One holiday season, we went to a wedding. I was about 4 years old. I was getting antsy, so Dick and Jane gave me a sip of champagne, hoping that it would make me sleepy. Well, boy were they wrong! I started dancing around and swinging my skirt up, even right in front of the priest who married the newlyweds. Cheers to you!

Vacations

Two of our most popular places to take vacations each year was Big Bear and Rancho Mirage (near Palm Springs). We went to Big Bear each winter to go skiing and snowboarding. We had so much fun watching the boys learn how to ski and snowboard. It was always great to get up into the snow and the boys would have so much fun having snowball fights and building snowmen. One thing about skiing with young children, though, is all the gear you have to carry! When they're young, they can't carry much so you end up carrying their stuff along with yours and they need snacks and waters, so you're carrying all that too. All the while you're trudging along in those oh-so-comfortable ski boots.

I remember when they first learned to ski. We enrolled them in half-day ski school for three days in a row. They would take lessons in the morning then we would ski with them in the afternoon. After the first two days there wasn't much improvement. But that third day was the ticket. That afternoon they flew down the mountain with complete confidence and their form looked so good. I was so proud of them! Then skiing got really fun with them because they liked it so much better and it was fun to watch them.

In Big Bear you're never quite sure how much snow there will be year-to-year. Some years there's barely any snow on the mountain and the ski resort has to make snow. Every so often we get a great year where the mountain gets dumped on. This happened one particular year when we got lots of precipitation and cold temperatures in February after an unseasonably warm and dry January. We planned to go up the second weekend in February since the boys had that Monday off school. Once we got there, it started snowing and it never stopped during our trip. This was the first time the boys and I have skied in falling snow and it was fun, although very cold at times. On our second day, we had white-out conditions. That was a bit scary and we took a break in the lodge for a while.

When we left, unbeknownst to us, we were about to drive right into a full-blown blizzard on our way down the mountain. We were told by the front desk that we had a 1-2 hour window before the storm would hit. Well they were misinformed. This was the scariest driving conditions I have ever been in my life. We had to stop on the road three times to wipe off the windshield and pick ice off the windshield wipers. The turnouts were full of snow, so you literally had to just stop on the road and hope and pray that nobody slammed into you. Unfortunately, this storm was very cold so the snow level fell to 2500'! That barely ever happens in Southern California. We had snow the complete time we were coming down the mountain. Once we were on level ground, it was still snowing. I have never been so glad to finally see rain.

We would usually try to take a trip to Rancho Mirage in the desert in summer. We started this because the rates go down in the summer and even though it can get ungodly hot (it was 114° one year), you spend all your time in the pool anyway and during the middle of the day, you just go into your air-conditioned room for a couple of hours. And the evenings are wonderful – hot and dry.

One year, air pollution conditions were so bad in LA, Orange and San Diego counties because there were an unprecedented number of fires burning in all three counties that schools kept the children inside during recess and lunch and sports activities were cancelled for about a week. That weekend the prospect of staying inside the house for two days with boys who had had no physical activity for a week did not thrill us. We decided to escape to the desert because they had better air quality and we could actually be outdoors. So we packed up and left for the weekend. It was such a fun trip because it was so impromptu. We really shouldn't have spent the money, but we just wanted them to be able to play. They had so much fun splashing in the pool all weekend and we had fun relaxing and watching them. It is one of our most fun vacation memories.

We took our first major trip with them to Hawaii. We waited until they were old enough to really appreciate it and until we had enough frequent-flyer miles to fly all four of us there. The pool area was a child's paradise. And what is a child's paradise is a parent's paradise too. There were different pools all connected by a waterway, a cave, a couple of waterfalls and a big slide. I had fun swimming in all those pools, too. However, the big waterfall was a little too fast for me. Not for the boys, though. Funny, you almost would never know there was a beach around with the amount of time we stayed at the pool.

One day, though, we went to the beach to find a sign that said it was closed because of a shark sighting. It turned out that they had to keep that beach closed for three days while two sharks kept swimming up and down the coast very close to shore. Scary – and kind of cool. So, it was a good thing the pool was so enticing. We didn't do much sight-seeing because David and I had done that the first time we came to the island (Maui) and found out it's much nicer to just enjoy the scenery and relax.

Another big trip we took was to Yosemite. What a beautiful place! We stayed at a hotel about 15 minutes outside of the park. On both of these trips we went during the end of September to the beginning of October because the boys attended year-round school and were on break then. We were able to hike and see all the splendor of the valley without having to deal with the crowds. The only downside was that most of the waterfalls were dried up by that time. We watched deer roaming and eating both in the valley and at our hotel. It was cool to be so close to them. The boys kept hoping we would see a bear, but we were secretly glad we didn't.

On our last day of vacation, we planned to take the boys fishing for their first time at Bass Lake, which was close. It rained, so instead we went to the indoor swimming pool at the hotel. It was cool that the hotel had that, and it kept the boys happy. We got lucky, however, because the rain let up and the sun came out. So, we ended up going to Bass Lake for afternoon fishing. Bass Lake is beautiful!! It looks like a lake in the Alpine Mountains. Beautiful pine trees surround the lake and it is pristine and sparkling. The boys were both successful in catching their first fish and had a memorable time.

The summer of Zach's 10th birthday, we decided to go up to Northern California to visit family and friends. My oldest brother had a house close to the American River which is popular for white-water river rafting. So, we decided to do something different and try rafting. We loved it!! Absolutely loved it! It was fun, thrilling, but not terrifying and we had times when we got to jump into the river, which was great because the temperature reached 111° that day! Also, the scenery was beautiful! It was a great activity to do together as a family; a great way to spend some time together.

The next fall, during their fall break, we went to the Grand Canyon and Las Vegas. Unbelievably, I had never been to the Grand Canyon although I've lived in Southern California most of my life, so it's always been fairly close. The Grand Canyon is absolutely breathtaking! Pictures just can't do it justice – you have to actually experience it. We got up the first morning and walked on the rim to see the sunrise – it was spectacular! Then, we drove around the canyon and stopped at various lookout points to get different views of it. From some lookout points, you can look down the canyon all the way to the Colorado River. While we were checking out different lookouts, it started raining. By the time we were finished and going back to our hotel, it had become a thunderstorm. We spent the rest of the afternoon on a patio at the hotel's restaurant, eating lunch and watching a fantastic lightning show off the walls of the Grand Canyon!

We also hiked down part of a trail near our hotel. We kept passing riders on mules who were coming from the bottom of the canyon. We asked a few of them if they enjoyed themselves and the unanimous response was "it's something you only need to do once in your lifetime". Almost all of them looked tired and sore.

Then we went to Las Vegas, which was a first for the boys. They loved all the lights and being able to stay up late. They also enjoyed riding in a cab for the first time. They wanted to try a limo, but that wasn't in our budget. During the day, we would spend time at the hotel pool and that part seemed like one of our desert getaways. But then you would walk into the hotel and hear all the rings and dings of the casino. David and I have been to Vegas a number of times and neither one of us are big gamblers (thankfully). Suffice to say, the boys were a lot more taken with Vegas than we were. But now they've experienced it.

Dick and Jane Moment

Speaking of Vegas, our family took a trip there when I was about 10 years old. The family wanted to go around town and show us kids Circus Circus, while my parents did some gambling. I got sick, however, and couldn't leave the hotel room. So the family left me there, with a couple of comic books, while they perused the town. Maybe things were safer back then, but I shudder now to even think about having left Zach or Alex in a hotel room in Vegas by themselves!

Birthdays

Ask many mothers and they will tell you how involved and stressful kids' birthdays can get. I'm not talking about big, fancy, blown-out parties either. Just getting a bunch of kids together and throwing a party. It was easier when the boys celebrated their first birthdays, although it was still stressful because you want everything to go well since it's such a big milestone. You know, however, that if things go wrong and if (when) your child starts crying, they will never remember it. You can selectively keep the photos that tell a story of a perfect event. When they're turning one, they don't really have any friends yet so it's really a family affair with lots of adults and you don't have to worry about entertaining a big group of kids.

By the time they're in preschool or kindergarten, you end up having a party where everyone in the class is invited so no one feels left out. Also, at that age the parties tend to be co-ed – girls' and boys' interests are very similar then. These parties can have around 20 kids and usually a parent accompanies them since they are so young. Because of the quantity of people, these parties were usually held off-site, at places like Chuck E. Cheese's, Pump It Up, a local gymnastics studio, etc. These parties are wild, with 20 kids running/jumping around, then eating pizza and cake. After a couple of years, all of us parents have been to these places multiple times. You're happy when your child receives a birthday invitation because you know they'll be excited and have fun, but then you realize you have to endure a couple of hours of dizzying noise and movement.

We are fortunate to have a lot of family living near us and when the parties started to become big kid affairs at these venues, we decided to have separate friend birthday parties from the family-oriented events. So now we had two parties to host and they were both on a weekend to accommodate everyone's schedule. Now you add up food and drinks for both parties, two cakes, decorations, party favors, etc. and you're dropping several hundred dollars for parties that are not lavish. Don't even get me started on party favors. By the time you put together party bags for the kids to take home, you've spent at least $5/bag. For twenty kids, you've just spent $100 on party favors! And that's if you manage to keep it at $5/bag.

By the end of the weekend, you're spent. The house is a mess, there are toys and their boxes in different piles and you're dreading looking at the next month's credit card statement. However, you've got a very happy youngster who had a great time being the center of attention all weekend. So, in short, it's worth it. Now you have your child's actual birthday, where you bring cupcakes or party favors or something to the whole class at school and we always had a tradition in our household where you got to choose what to have for dinner.

It gets easier as they get older. One year, Zach just decided to invite one friend to Disneyland on his birthday. Another year he just invited a few friends to go bowling and I brought cupcakes and a small gift to give each child when they left. Alex decided that for his tenth birthday, he would rather just have a chunk of money from us instead of a party with friends. He wanted to save up for an iPad. We still had the family parties for them, but as they got older, we decided to have these only for "big" birthdays (eg. 10, 13, 16, etc.) When the kids were young, they loved having a lot of presents to open. Now they like getting gift cards and money so they can put it all together and go buy something big they really want.

Dick and Jane Moment

My birthday is fairly close to Halloween, so Jane started having my birthday parties on Halloween and taking my friends and me trick-and-treating. It was actually ingenious because we always had fun and my mom had a built-in way to keep us occupied.

Seasons

Fall has always been my favorite season. I like the crispness of the air, the light gets more dramatic and the colors seem richer. Fall starts out the exciting holiday season. Also, school traditionally starts in the fall and I've always liked the new beginning that that provides. Since having children, I've enjoyed sharing the holidays and the beginning of school with them. It's fun to watch them enjoying these milestones. It has made this time of year a lot busier than I used to be, though. So, by the end of fall I'm sometimes starting to get a bit harried and tired and I still have Christmas to get through.

I do like winter and always have, although it does sometimes get old when it keeps getting dark by 5 p.m. One of the reasons I enjoy winter is that I've always lived in California, where they are mild. The biggest holiday for us in winter is Christmas. Christmas is such a fun holiday when you have children because you love to watch them enjoy all of it: going to see Santa, picking out and decorating a tree, decorating the house, baking cookies, opening presents, visiting relatives, etc. It also gets very harried with buying all the gifts, helping out at school parties, cooking, baking, visiting relatives, having friends and relatives visit us and such.

The week between Christmas and New Year's kind of feels like a holiday hangover, as you try to clean up left-over wrapping paper, pine cones, throw out boxes, try to figure out where you're going to put all the kids' new toys and try to figure out which old toys can be given away. Then you have New

Year's Eve and Day and then it feels like a bit of a let-down as everyone goes back to everyday life after all the excitement and festivities. However now with children, we usually go skiing so that gives us something to look forward to and makes winter much more exciting. I love going up to the mountains and experiencing the snow - that makes me feel it truly is winter.

Spring is always a feel-good season as the weather gets warmer and the days get longer. There seems to be a more carefree feeling in the air. With children it's fun to be able to get out with them more and do more outside activities. Sometimes we'll have a picnic dinner in the school's field near our house or at the pool. The kids start getting excited about the upcoming end of the year and it can start to get harder to get them to do their homework because they see the end in sight and they're yearning for it.

Summer is my least-favorite season although I liked it as a child. I do remember getting bored with it though by mid-August. I don't like a lot of heat unless I'm on vacation near a pool and/or a beach. It's just not that fun having to run around and do errands and chores when it's really hot and the sun's beating down on you. I do like it more now, though, that I have children. They love it and I like watching them at the pool or the beach. I feel like a kid again when they entice me into the ocean for some body-surfing. They love being able to sleep in (I do, too) and not having to worry about homework (I do, too). The evenings are also wonderful because it's still nice and warm without being stifling. It's fun to go out to the pool for awhile after dinner and just watch the boys swim and play.

Traditions

I've always liked to make minor holidays special and festive. I like to make tacos on Cinco de Mayo and, of course, I've GOT to make corned beef and cabbage on St. Patrick's Day – I'm Irish. But I also like to make a French meal on Bastille Day (July 14), have unhealthy appetizers on Superbowl Sunday, make something elegant on Valentine's Day, prepare something German during Oktoberfest ,etc. I just think it's fun to make events out of certain dates and for me, that usually means what I'm going to cook. So, here's a rundown of traditions we would have for minor holidays during the year.

As mentioned above, I love to make some unhealthy appetizers for Superbowl Sunday. The boys haven't been excited about football yet, so I was hoping to entice them to watch with us by making dips, nachos, hot dogs and a favorite of mine – stuffed potato skins. They would take some food and go upstairs to watch Cartoon Network – oh well.

On Valentine's Day I always give each son a heart-shaped box of chocolates. It's a tradition that my father started with me and I loved it so I keep it up with Zach and Alex. Then I think of something elegant to make for dinner, like Cornish Game Hens with a raspberry-Chambord sauce – yum!

For St. Patrick's Day, we begin the day by discovering that the water in the toilet bowls have turned green. Ah, the mischievous leprechauns have been visiting. Then the boys have fun watching as David pours milk in their cups and the milk magically turns green!! (The magic of a secret drop of green food coloring, that is.) All day, we think we see leprechauns running to hide and make mischief and every once in awhile, one of us gets pinched. Dinner has to be corned beef and cabbage, and some boiled potatoes. The luck of the Irish to ya!

For Cinco de Mayo, it's fun to have tacos and let everyone make their own. The boys really love this! I just set everything out and they think it's fun to build their own. We listen to Mexican music as we eat.

For Bastille Day, I try different French foods. Sometimes we'll do more of a picnic thing and have Brie, pate, a baguette, some salad, etc. Other times I might make something like Coq Au Vin. The boys aren't particularly fond of Bastille Day but I'm a Francophile so they have to endure.

Now we also have a couple of "everyday" traditions – or should I say, "every week" traditions. One of our favorites is popcorn night. We started this when the boys were toddlers. Every Friday night, the boys would pick a video (it was videos back then!) and I would make popcorn with an air-popcorn popper (do you remember those things?) that I had since college! That thing cost about $10 over a decade ago and it still works. We would spread out an old sheet on the living room carpet and I would keep making bowls of popcorn until everyone was full. We used to watch a lot of *Land Before Time* movies – I miss those. As the boys have gotten older, we've progressed to *Star Wars* movies and now they sometimes just want to watch shows on TV. But they always look forward to popcorn nights and have now started to invite their friends over to join us.

Another weekly tradition is me making pancakes from scratch on Sunday mornings. In the summer when fresh blueberries are in season, I'll sometimes add blueberries to the batter. I would like to try bananas and pecans, but the boys aren't excited about that yet. I've added apples, but they weren't too keen on that either. When I added chocolate chips, that was it!! They loved it! Now

I'm always making chocolate chip pancakes. To keep things interesting, I usually try to make the pancakes in different shapes according to the time of year. I'll make Christmas trees around Christmas, hearts near Valentine's Day, skis and snowboards if we have a ski trip planned soon, presents near someone's birthday, etc. We make a game of seeing whether they can guess what shape the pancakes are supposed to be when they first get to the table. We have quite a laugh at some of my less successful designs – I'm really not very artistic, as is sometimes very apparent.

Dick and Jane Moment

After my parents divorced, my brothers and I would spend Christmas Eve with Jane and Christmas day with Dick. Jane didn't have much money, so we began a tradition. We would buy a Christmas tree on Christmas Eve. The prices were always slashed and the pickin's were slim. So, we would look for a sorry, Charlie Brown-type of tree that we would then bring home and lovingly decorate – sweet tradition.

Making Memories

Right now, I'm feeling nostalgic about Thanksgiving and the upcoming holiday season. I remember a few years ago when I was volunteering in Zach's class before Thanksgiving. The teacher was talking about all the wonderful smells as the Thanksgiving meal is being prepared. We had always gone to a relative's house for Thanksgiving. So, I started to feel sad and a bit guilty that my sons hadn't ever experienced all those wonderful smells at our house. I decided I would cook a turkey dinner the day after Thanksgiving. I don't remember too much of it, but I did cook the meal and it came out well and was delicious.

I've done this at least one more time since then. The problem is that no one remembers it. The boys don't even remember me ever cooking a Thanksgiving meal and my husband and me have a vague recollection of it. So, the main reason for doing this, so the boys would have fond memories of all the wonderful aromas, has completely eluded us. I thought about preparing this meal again this year and talked to my husband about it, but we just laughed, as we realized it probably wouldn't be remembered, either.

During the holidays this year, I made pumpkin bread, some green chocolate chip cookies (more details on that later) and some gingerbread for the first time. One of the reasons for doing this was to fill the house with all those wonderful smells of the season so the boys could remember how nice our house smelled over the holidays. I've done some of this in previous holidays too, but I'm not really a baker so it doesn't come easy for me. For example, I don't even own a rolling pin and hate the mess of flouring a surface and rolling cookie dough on it to cut out shapes with cookie cutters. It's just so much easier to buy the cookies at the store. They're abundant this time of year and they all look really festive and delicious. It's easier for me to infuse the smell of the holidays with breads, like pumpkin or gingerbread. I will make drop cookies because those don't involve too much mess.

Now will the boys remember these goodies and the sweet, spicy smells they imbued our house with? I hope so. But the truth is, I don't know. In the future I guess I better take a picture of it. That won't capture the smells, but at least it will prove that I did make delicacies over the holidays.

About those green chocolate chip cookies – before Thanksgiving Zach's grade had a potluck lunch where everyone was supposed to bring something that represented their ethnicity. We've had these lunches throughout the years, so I know them well.

The boys are a hodgepodge of ethnicities and the easiest one to bring food for is Irish – I usually make mashed potatoes. Well, the teachers had let the children decide what group of food to bring (entrée, side, dessert, etc.) Zach chose a dessert. I thought, "what Irish dessert am I going to bring?" I tried to change it to a side dish so I could bring the aforementioned mash potatoes, but the teacher wouldn't let us change. I researched some different Irish desserts and gave Zach a few ideas. But then I thought, "everybody loves chocolate chip cookies – I could just dye them green." Zach loved that idea.

Honestly, I didn't know if it would work. I didn't know if it would turn into some weird color since chocolate chip cookies are light brown and combining that with green could turn into a mess. So when I made the cookies, the recipe called for white sugar and brown sugar. I decided to use white sugar only, so the cookies would be lighter and therefore the green dye would take better.

Well it did work out and the cookies came out a bit sweeter than usual. I thought brown sugar was sweeter than white, but I guess it's the other way around. Well it was a hit with the kids – they loved it! I ended up making about 100 cookies (3 classes of about 32 students each) and they were all eaten. The kids did not care that they were a bit too sweet, in fact they liked it more. Now hopefully my kids will remember that (I kept some cookies at home).

Funny thing is when Alex got to this grade, he picked dessert also. But he decided he wanted me to bake a cake because not only is he Irish, but his birthday is the day before St. Patrick's Day, so there's a birthday connection with him being Irish as well. He wanted chocolate cake with chocolate frosting dyed green. I explained to him that chocolate frosting was not going to take green dye well and persuaded him it was best for me to use white frosting. It turned out well and all the kids loved it (it's cake of course), so it's kind of funny that both my children picked desserts for that ethnic feast when Irish food isn't known for its desserts – so much for the mashed potatoes!

Capturing Those Memories

I have never been a person who takes a lot of pictures, but once you have children you realize you need to capture special moments like birthdays, holidays, vacations, performances and just snapshots of them as they're growing up. David has been the main picture-taker in our family since it doesn't come naturally to me. I get wrapped up in the moment and forget to pick up the camera. However, I did get better at this because David started to realize that he wasn't in many of our pictures and thought some day, the boys might forget what he looked like (ha ha).

I was good at getting the pictures printed and put into photo albums when the boys were younger, and I'm glad I did! Because now, about the last ten years' worth of pictures are either in big bags full of photo envelopes, on a digital disk with more than 900 pictures or somewhere in the Cloud. Life has just gotten busier, more complicated and hectic as they've gotten older.

When it comes to videotaping, we have taped certain important events like some of their plays and musical performances and some holiday celebrations. One thing I don't like about it, though, is that I don't feel as though I'm experiencing the moment as well while I'm looking through the camera or phone. It makes it feel a bit more distant. So, I try to pull myself away from it every so often so I can take in the scene.

One memorable event we taped recently was a performance from the classes in Alex's grade. Each class had a scene to do and some kids also performed certain songs or dances. Alex sang with a small group of his friends. He told us before the performance that he didn't want us to tape it. However, we told him we had to because we wanted a copy of it, especially because he was going to be singing in a small group.

When his group was up on the stage, he saw David videotaping. During his singing, he shook his head at David and motioned for him to stop taping. Then he would go back into character and continue singing. He kept doing this throughout the song. Parents were chuckling, it looked so cute! (He would hate that!). So many parents came up to us after the show was over and even days afterward and told us how funny that was! Now we have bribe material on him for the future!

Dick and Jane Moment

We had a huge Saint Bernard dog named Timothy and another named Hannah. They had a couple of litters and we took a video of one of the litters being let out of the garage to be fed. We would have to put the puppies (about 8 of them) in the garage while we set out their bowls of food. Then we would open the door and they would come running out, tripping over each other excitedly, trying to get to the food. A swarm of cute, little puppies running as fast as they can and pushing each other out of the way to get food – very cute!

Feeding the Beasts

Healthy Living

I never wanted to be crazy when it comes to nutrition because I feel that ultimately makes your children crave the foods that have been forbidden and as they get older, they will have a harder time limiting their consumption of them. I also realized that while they were very young, most of their exposure to foods and healthy habits, like exercise, would come from David and me. I knew that once they started school, they would be increasingly influenced by the foods at the cafeteria and other students' lunches and snacks. So, I controlled what I could early-on, slowly relaxing my standards as they got exposed to less-than-completely-healthy influences.

When Zach and Alex were babies ready to start solid foods, I started them with rice baby food and then introduced them to different vegetables. I introduced green vegetables before the sweeter orange vegetables, so they could get a taste for them without developing a preference right away for the sweeter flavors. Once I felt comfortable that they would eat baby food consisting of peas, green beans, even broccoli, I introduced carrots and sweet potatoes. Once they were eating a variety of these easily, I slowly introduced different fruits.

I'm so glad I did this because they would always eat vegetables as well as fruit. Some other mothers would tell me that their children would only eat fruit and shun vegetables. Through asking them questions, I found out that they had introduced foods to their children in no particular order, so the babies ended up leaning towards the sweeter flavors. To this day, my children are fairly good about eating vegetables as well as fruit. Although I do have to admit that we've lost some headway now with the influence of foods from other kids, fast food and school.

Regarding fast food, I held out as long as I could. Eventually, though, your children will want cheeseburgers, fries, chicken nuggets, etc. because they see other children eating them or have seen these products in commercials on TV. So they eventually tried a variety of fast food, but I would always buy the smallest sizes and I tried to keep them from and then limit their consumption of sodas (more on that later). Also, I tried to stay away from "Happy Meals" for as long as possible. I knew that once that started, they would always want them and there would be a plethora of cheap little toys strewn all over the house. Of course, it did eventually happen. That started a whole other problem as they would fight over which toy they got or start crying when they didn't get the toy they wanted. Then I tried to make sure they got the same toy, but then they complained they didn't want the same thing. You just can't win with those "Happy Meals" or whatever name each chain gives to them. Please tell me I'm not the only mother who has driven to a couple of different places because the first one didn't have the right selection of toys.

When it comes to sodas, I held off as long as possible on that also. I've read numerous articles about how drinking sodas can really make you gain weight because you don't realize how many calories you're consuming since the body doesn't feel as satisfied with liquid calories as it does with solid ones and that the high-fructose corn syrup in sodas spikes insulin levels. I also limited juice because it's really not very healthful either and you're better off just eating a piece of fruit. So, in the beginning Zach and Alex mostly drank milk and water. I taught them that if they were really thirsty, say after running around, that water was the best drink to quench their thirst. I usually didn't have juice or sodas at our house unless I needed to bring juices for a snack after sports games or we were having a party of some sort. Therefore, juice and soda became drinks they had once in awhile. I didn't limit them so much that they would go crazy for these, I just didn't have them so readily available, so they got used to regularly consuming milk and water.

The other day I took Zach and Alex to a local farm stand. I thought they could pick out whatever fruits and vegetables that might look good or interesting to them. I figured this would get them more excited about eating these items. I forgot that this stand also carried candy and chips near the registers to increase impulse buys, like every other grocery store. So, what did my children gravitate towards? Of course. I kept having to say "no, no, no" to all the requests for different candy and chips, but at least I did get them to say yes to some strawberries and kiwifruit.

When it comes to exercise, I try to make sure they get some every day. Sometimes it's hard, but we always make sure they're signed up for some type of sport or activity. If it happens to be a time where there's a lull, I'll try to take them swimming, go to the beach, ride bikes or just run around in a park. David and I also try to show them how important exercising is by letting them know that it is an important part of our lives. Recently, we've started playing tennis together. This is great because it's an activity we can all do together and we get a lot of exercise, especially bending down to get all the balls we've missed. We also like to go on hikes and sometimes kayak together. Also, when we go on vacation, we sometimes try new activities that are exercise-oriented. For example, we've tried white-water rafting and horseback riding. These are activities we don't regularly get to do at home and they're fun to experience together. The great thing about exercising as a family is that you get to visit and bond with each other while you're taking care of yourself. You also build some fun family memories.

I also try not to always use food as a reward because I don't want to set them up for future food issues. It's so easy and quick to use food as a reward. However, I try to do other things like give them more time watching TV or being on digital devices. I try not to do this too often either because these are passive activities that don't translate to good health. So, then I thought of other rewards such as money (they always want to buy more toys), playing a game with them, reading to them for longer at bedtime, having a friend over and things like that. This isn't to say that I never use food as a reward, I just try to balance it with more positive things.

I was so proud when Zach's fourth grade class did a project on California agriculture. They each had to pick a product grown in California. Zach picked artichokes. I was proud of that because both boys really like artichokes and I *love* them. I really think I influenced them there because David doesn't care for them, but I made them for the boys years ago and tried to make them seem fun (peel off each leaf and dip into melted butter until you get to the great part, the heart, then cut that up and dip it into melted butter – YUM!)

Anyway, part of the project was to include a recipe for the product. I wanted to do something more creative than artichoke dip, which I don't like anyway because I don't like mayonnaise. I looked for ideas for days and searched the internet for ideas. I finally came across a recipe for something called Artichoke Gratinata. You basically sauté artichoke hearts with garlic, Italian parsley and some red pepper flakes. Then you put it into a baking dish and cover it with bread crumbs mixed with melted butter and parmesan cheese. You then bake it in a 450° oven for about 10-15 minutes until the top gets crispy. I was so proud when Zach tried it and loved it. I brought it to his class and believe it or not, it was a hit!! The kids liked it. I'm sure the crunchy topping with cheese helped. Anyway, I had only one serving left to bring home and later that day when Zach saw there was more left over, he was excited and asked to have the rest for a snack. I was proud of him – he was excited about a healthy snack!

Dick and Jane Moment

Jane was into health food, even working at a health store at one time. So, in the effort to keep my brothers and me as healthy as possible, she would give us vitamins. We would take them (or should I say try to take them) every morning. Trouble was, they were huge – we called them horse pills. We would be trying to drink enough water to get them down and inevitably someone would choke, and the horse pill with copious amounts of water would get spewn all over the kitchen floor. But, she would just keep giving them to us – we hated it.

Cooking Used to Be One of My Hobbies

I remember David and I used to watch a show on the Food Network that I really loved. The guy was a chef from Florida and most of his recipes were fish dishes. I love fish and love to find new ways to cook it. I used to love watching this show early Saturday afternoons and deciding what we were going to have for dinner based on inspiration I got from watching his cooking. Then I'd go buy the ingredients and enjoy trying to turn it into the picture I saw on the set earlier. There was no stress, no real timetable – we ate whenever it was ready. I would sip a glass of wine while I cooked and many times we would eat an appetizer before.

Well as you can guess, dinners don't look like this anymore. Now I have to plan meals a week in advance – forget last-minute inspiration. I want to grocery shop as little as possible because now it's just one more chore for me to do. So, the week's meals need to be planned and I'll pick up extra perishables sometime during the middle of the week when needed. I also need to watch our budget so the meal planning also includes looking at weekly specials at a couple of neighborhood stores.

When I'm cooking during the week and even on weekends, I'm stressed - the boys are hungry and I'm trying to time everything to be done a few minutes after David gets home from work, not before and not too long after or we're eating too late and the boys will keep rummaging through the cupboards and refrigerator. The tediousness of day-after-day cooking, planning, cleaning and trying to figure out yet another way to cook chicken just seems to take most the fun and creativity out of cooking. So, I find a hobby I used to have is no longer one.

That's not to say that I never get pleasure out of cooking. Sometimes on the weekends I want to cook something special and I do get pleasure out of it. I also enjoy looking forward to eating the spoils of my work. For example, sometimes I make Cornish Game Hen. I like making this dish and working on the raspberry/Chambord sauce that I'll serve with it. Sometimes I like to make food to go along with a fun event. For example, I love to make a variety of different appetizers for watching the Academy Awards. I'll make stuffed mushrooms, smoked salmon with cream cheese and chives on crackers or potato chips, shrimp cocktail, sautéed asparagus, etc. – whatever strikes my fancy. I have fun planning it, preparing it and the most fun eating it while watching the show and sipping champagne. So, I guess my hobby isn't gone entirely, it just doesn't come out as often as it used too.

Dick and Jane Moment

Dick was known as a gourmet cook. He enjoyed it and even had an article written about him in a local newspaper. When I was 18, I asked him to teach me how to make some of his dishes, like Coquilles St. Jacques, Coq au Vin, etc. However, I was horrified when he mentioned that one of the ingredients in one of his recipes was a jar of baby food meat! I can't even remember which dish it was, I was so grossed out! So much for him teaching me how to cook.

Meal Time (But You Liked That Last Week)

This is one issue that really drives me crazy. It's hard enough to expand the repertoire of items they will eat, but it's really aggravating when they just seem to randomly change it. When my boys were younger and still very fussy about food, I would make two dinners many times. A lot of the time it would be a version of what I was making for David and me, but not always. I would still expose them to new foods and coax them to try them since they say that children need to be presented with new food items a number of times before they might develop a taste for it.

Then I started making two dinners less and less because it was a pain and they were getting to ages where they needed to like more foods. When they wouldn't eat the dinner in front of them, I made them at least try it then they could pour themselves a bowl of cereal, although none of that sugary stuff. If I had sugary cereals in the house (because sometimes they begged and begged), I told them that it was a dessert. Anyway, I digress. At least I knew if they had cereal, they would be eating something healthful.

I finally got to the point where there were a number of healthy dinners that they would not only eat, but enjoy. They enjoyed beef, chicken, pork, fish (yes, fish), artichokes, corn, carrots, hamburgers (of course), tacos, chili, ham and white bean soup, stir fry, chicken noodle casserole and even linguine and clams (I was really proud of that). But then a funny thing started happening. I would confidently serve these family classics that they always enjoyed, and they would complain! They wouldn't like it anymore! What's up with that?! It wasn't as if I kept serving the same stuff over and over so they got tired of it. Their taste buds just changed and were going back to being fussier. I'm still dealing with this now and it really aggravates me. Yesterday I served linguine and clams and Zach complained about it while Alex refused to eat it – he ate cereal instead. They used to have second helpings of it! I don't get it. Maybe next time I'll make it for David and me and have them watch us eat it while they're eating leftover chicken or something. Maybe then they'll appreciate it.

Snacks, Snacks and More Snacks

Nowadays it seems everywhere you turn someone is handing kids snacks. You can't go to the park, pool or beach without packing some snacks. Preschoolers and kindergarteners break for snack time. Kids in grade school bring snacks for recess or buy them in the cafeteria. After any type of meeting or sports practice or game, there are snacks. There were times when my sons would have a Cub Scout meeting then have some sort of sports practice after that. On those days, they would get two sets of snacks. I would try to limit them, but they saw what the other kids were eating and wanted some. Of course, the snacks are seldom healthy. What mom wants to be the one who brings the "healthy" snacks. The kids would be disappointed and your child would be embarrassed.

Also, it usually turned out that the snacks had to be two items and a juice – one item wasn't enough, in case a kid didn't like it. So, our kids get used to having junky snacks and juice every time they get together with other kids. Of course, if you have a play date at your house, there needs to be snacks. One problem with all this occurred when the event ended right before you were going home to dinner. Now you are filling your hungry child up with junk right before mealtime. One mom and I tried to stop this at one point and were told that the kids expected it. Of course, we were told this by a father (sheesh!) During their soccer games, we were expected to provide the kids with a snack during half-time! At least it was always some type of fruit – they didn't get the crap until after the game. Anyway, I'm going to go take a break now … and get a snack.

Dick and Jane Moment

The first time my husband went to Jane's house while we were dating, she had spread out some snacks on the patio, like cheese, salami, crackers, etc. My brother, Brian, happened to be there also. When she went back into the house to get something, Brian picked everything up, threw it away and replaced it with items he had bought. David watched with his mouth wide open. Brian explained that he was just trying to keep us from getting sick, as Jane had a penchant of serving well-expired food.

I Don't Bake (Much)

I'm a cook, not a baker. It seems to me that most people fall into one of these two camps, if they cook at all. You either like cooking better than baking or the other way around. The reason I prefer cooking is that it is creative and not exact. I tend to not follow recipes word for word, changing things here or there as I see fit. I also generally don't use exact measurements when cooking – I throw in a pinch here or a pour there. I judge what I want to add and how much by taste, aroma and look. However, baking is a chemical reaction. Therefore, it requires you to use exact measurements or it won't come out correctly. That's exactly what I don't like about it.

Since I don't bake much, most of the times I've needed to bring baked goods to a function (school, Cub Scouts, etc.), I would usually buy it at the store. Every birthday cake has been from a bakery or Baskin Robbins. Part of that is also because I feel I wouldn't decorate it well enough. I have baked occasionally when Zach and Alex have specifically requested it. For example, I do remember baking cupcakes for one of Alex's birthdays. He really wanted me to and wanted to make sure it was chocolate cake with chocolate frosting. Then he wanted me to bake a cake for a school event. Mind you, I don't even own a cake pan. I called up one of my mom friends for help and she suggested I buy a plastic cake pan from the store. They actually have really nice plastic pans with covers, so you can easily transport the finished product.

Beyond these examples, I have baked banana bread and pumpkin bread a few times and those came out well. I've also baked cookies, but not as often as I should have. To be honest, I did make pancakes almost every Sunday morning, but that's not baking per se because you're cooking them on a griddle. So, my kids can't say I didn't make any sweet treats for them – I just didn't bake them that often. I was lucky that my children's school never made a big deal about items being homemade. I can't imagine what that pressure would be like. Well, I'm going to go now and bake a batch of chocolate chip cookies because now I'm feeling guilty that there hasn't been the smell of freshly baked goods in our house enough.

Reflections

The Days Are Long, But the Years Are Short

I was a bit frustrated when I first heard this when I was a new mother because I was pretty frantic during that time. My first son had colic for 6 months. I'm talking colic where just about every moment he was awake that he wasn't feeding, he was screaming. I was a nervous mess. I couldn't take him anywhere because if he woke up, he would start screaming. I didn't always want to shove a bottle at him because I was concerned about future weight issues. He didn't like pacifiers and picking him up, rocking him, singing to him, rubbing his belly, nothing seemed to work. Believe me, I read a lot, talked to his pediatrician, tried different dietary changes and nothing worked. But I knew I needed to hear this adage even though to me at that time, the days were VERY long. I would try to put it all in perspective. I also tried to do this when his brother was born 20 months later and now I was taking care of a newborn and a toddler. It would get very hectic especially when they both needed me at once.

However, listening to this adage and trying to remember it, did change me in certain ways. I made sure to rock them in our rocking chair often. I made a ritual of reading nursery rhymes to them and then taking turns laying in each of their beds while singing bedtime songs. It didn't matter that I made up words to a couple of the songs. To this day if they hear the correct version, they'll probably think "hey, that's not right. That's not the way mom sang it." It helped me during bath time, when water started splashing all over the floor and I was getting tired of how long it was taking. “Take a breath” I would tell myself. There will be a day when you won’t be watching them bathe themselves anymore.

As they got older and started elementary school, I volunteered in each of their classrooms each week. I enjoyed getting to see them in the school environment and they loved having me there. I knew there would come a time when they didn’t want me to be at school anymore, so I took advantage of it. I also liked the fact that I got to know their classmates and their teachers more personally through working there each week. I walked Zach and Alex to and from school and visited with other moms as we were milling about the school yard.

As a family, we tried to watch every sports game Zach or Alex had, although sometimes they overlapped so I would watch one son’s game while David watched the other. But we would try to root each other on as much as possible. We also tried to have dinner together as many nights as possible, so we could spend time together and talk about the day.

On vacations when the boys were young, we would get a hotel room with two queen beds. Instead of the boys sleeping in one bed and David and me in the other, we would sleep one parent and one child in each bed, alternating the coupling. We did this because it was our opportunity to sleep with each of the boys and we knew the days of this would not be long. There would come a time when they wouldn’t want to sleep next to mom or dad. But we took advantage of the opportunity as much as possible (sorry to embarrass you guys).

Tonight, I’m going to a middle school information meeting for Zach. I can’t believe that he’s going to enter middle school soon. Although it was difficult at times, it did just seem a little while ago that he was just a little baby.

Activities

We tried so many types of activities and sports over the years because we wanted to expose Zach and Alex to as many opportunities as possible, so they could choose their individual interests. We tried sports such as baseball, basketball, football, soccer, swimming, tennis, tae kwon do, skiing/snowboarding, surfing, etc. We also exposed them to activities like Cub Scouts, various camps and after-school classes on building robots, filming movies, cartooning, etc. and various music lessons like cello, violin, guitar and vocal. Many of these activities didn't stick, but some lasted for years and gave them a good base and David and I did feel it was important to expose them to all these.

One issue that comes up when providing activities for your children is overscheduling. There were times when this happened to us. In particular, I remember one Fall when both boys were involved in soccer, swimming and Cub Scouts. They would each have four days of swim practice, two days of soccer practice, two weekend days of swim meets once a month, a game each on Saturday and a Cub Scout meeting once a week, plus sometimes Cub Scout activities on the weekends. It was crazy! It was a crazy schedule with one child, but imagine having to organize the schedule and drive two kids around. David and I would have to split up during the weekends to take turns watching games, swim meets and going to Cub Scout activities. Thankfully, the boys' homework wasn't too heavy back then. After that season, we limited the boys to two activities per season. There was so much going on that it became stressful for everyone and ceased to be fun. You want to give your kids lots of opportunities, but you don't want to burn them out (let alone yourself).

As the boys grew up, they started deciding which activities they were no longer interested in and many of these fell by the wayside. They also wanted and needed unscheduled time to just hang out with friends and goof off. Additionally, their homework became more time-consuming and demanding, especially in middle school. So, they ended up with a good sense of what they're interested in and we all learned a good balance for our family. Of course, we will keep offering them new opportunities as they arise, but we will always be aware of the dangers of being overscheduled.

Sibling Rivalry

Why, why, why do they always have to scream and fight? I swear they really do like each other. Really they do, even though they won't admit it and say that they hate each other (that really irks David and me). I mean they share a bedroom and they can't stop talking at night and you hear them talking to each other when they wake up. They like the same things and sometimes even share friends. Why then, do they have to fight pretty much EVERY SINGLE DAY!!!

We tell them how lucky they are to each have a brother. David tells them he always wanted a brother. I tell them I always wanted a sister. We each desired someone to play with. They have that, and they do play together well a lot. It's just that eventually something happens while playing where it turns into yelling and them sometimes hitting. Sometimes they just seem bored and one finds it fun to irritate the other. We try to explain that friends may come and go but that they will always have each other. We try to explain that they should work as a team – helping and encouraging each other, not just always putting each other down.

Today, Zach was gone all day to go to Legoland with a friend. I took Alex to a movie and then later one of his friends was going to come over (he couldn't make it to the movie). Unfortunately, his friend ended up getting sick and couldn't come over. I tried to find another friend to come over, but with such short notice, no one could. Alex got bored and I suggested going to play miniature golf, riding bikes, riding his scooter, practicing catch. He wasn't interested in any of that. As the afternoon wore on, he asked when Zach would be back. I thought that was sweet – he missed him. Once Zach came home, though, you guessed it – not five minutes passed before I heard them arguing and fighting. So much for them missing each other.

However, I do have to say they do have fun together also. That's why I don't completely understand their fighting. They share a room and we did that partially to help them build a stronger bond, although space was another factor. It does seem to work because they talk together at night, many times for too long and they talk to each other as they wake up first thing in the morning. I especially love weekend mornings when we're all sleeping in and David and I can hear them start to wake up and talk to each other. They can have a conversation for 15 or 20 minutes before they start getting out of bed. It's fun to hear them talking about the things they're both interested in – certain toys or TV shows. We can't always hear what they're saying but the sound of their voices and how animated they are is endearing. I hope these moments of the day really do cement their bond, while all the rest is just normal brother behavior.

Media Matters

When Zach and Alex were very young, I restricted their TV viewing to Sesame Street, maybe a cute PBS show now and then and sometimes a Baby Einstein video, especially when I needed to get dinner ready. I was careful about how much time they spent watching TV because all the professionals said that too much TV viewing was detrimental to young, developing minds. As they got older, they started watching more TV and mainstream channels, like Disney, Nickelodeon and Cartoon Network. I still limited how much they watched, but my restrictions became more lenient, especially when they would constantly be fighting and the one thing that seemed to distract them from that were certain shows. Also, as elementary-aged children, all their friends were watching the same shows, playing with the same toys and liked to talk all about it at school. If they weren't also watching these, they would be left out.

As they get older, the media issue gets trickier. They sometimes want to watch shows that David and I are not comfortable with. Sometimes they want to watch a show that's acceptable, but it stays on too late at night. They are also getting into music more and both now have iPods. So now lyrics are becoming an issue, although right now we are still able to control what they listen to since David loads the songs on their iPods. Websites are becoming more of an issue and social media will continue to as the become older, as well. They recently discovered YouTube and E-bay. We have to really restrict what they watch on YouTube and they have become avid shoppers on e-Bay, which obviously needs to be controlled.

Recently they wanted to see a new movie that was rated PG-13 because they like the lead actor. I read a review of the movie to see if there was any way it could be appropriate for them (I was already pretty sure it would be too much of a stretch, especially for Alex, being the younger of the two). The review talked about references to sex and teenage partying and I just knew it would introduce them to ideas they don't even know about yet. They were good about accepting the fact that it was for kids older than them, but it was interesting to see how much influence this one actor had on them.

They both got cellphones when they entered 4th grade. This was mostly a safety issue for us as we decided they could walk home from school alone once they were in 4th grade. We felt comfortable with this because we live about five minutes away, they don't have to cross any streets and as long as they had a cellphone with them, I could reach them if they took too long to get home or they could call me if something came up (which would happen periodically). When we first got them cellphones, they didn't have internet access. We just bought cheap phones with pay-as-you-go plans that allowed them a certain amount of money for a certain time period to use for calls and texts. They were both great about staying within the parameters of their plans because they knew if they ran out of money, they had to wait until the time period was up or buy more minutes themselves.

Another factor with all this media is that their time on these various items needs to be limited because it all adds up and takes away from other activities, like playing outside or interacting face-to-face. These items were off-limits for all of us during dinner, which means that even if our phone rang, we would just let the answering machine pick it up. Also, we stopped their use of all electronics after dinner during the week. The reason for this was twofold: first, they would get too involved and spend too much time with it in lieu of other things, like finishing homework, taking showers and reading. Second, it would stimulate them too much and make it harder for them to fall asleep. Instead, we would focus on finishing homework, showers, getting ready for bed and reading.

Tough Days

There are the inevitable tough days. One that happened recently was when my son came home and told me that his best friend told him he didn't want to hang out with him anymore. My son was really bummed about it and it really hurt me to see him feeling that way. I was worried how the next school day was going to be and tried to give him good advice, to make the day better. I also couldn't show him how much it upset me – that wouldn't help him at all, so I needed to seem like everything would be OK and it would get worked out, even if that meant he needed to find another friend or friends to hang out with.

I've also had days when I've needed to go to talk to the principal regarding my other son's behavior at school. This was never a fun proposition even though the principal was very nice and approachable. It's just something you don't want to have to do and I would be worried about it the night before. The next morning, I would just puff up my confidence, focus on trying to help my son and get my game face on.

Then there was the day when it was David's and my anniversary. We were going to go to dinner on Saturday evening and it was Wednesday, but I planned to make a nice dinner that evening. I just happened to have a meeting with both my sons' teachers after school that day – one of them was last-minute, after I received a phone call from her. Both meetings were not very good, especially the one with the teacher that I hadn't planned on meeting. I was frustrated with both boys after these meetings and talked to them as we walked home about how they needed to put more effort into their homework.

When we got home, they were supposed to start working right away on their homework, especially because of the meetings I had just had. They were hot, so I opened up our side door and then they started yelling. They were yelling about doing their homework right away and yelling at each other – they were bugging each other. Then I started yelling at them to just start their homework and for one of them to go upstairs. I told them to stop yelling and closed the side door. My blood was boiling at this point. I had had two bad meetings with their teachers, I was now fighting with them over homework, which shouldn't have been an issue and I had been running around doing errands all morning to get ready for our anniversary in the evening and hadn't had a chance to eat lunch yet (it was 2:45). On top of all of this, there is a knock on the door. If it isn't the police! A neighbor had called the police because of the yelling!

I was so shaken up and nervous. The police were very nice and one of them said he was the youngest of three boys, so he knows how it can get with the yelling and boys fighting. However, by the time my husband came home (early, and with flowers, no less), I was frazzled. I was trying to finish up laundry, help the boys with their homework and was told that one of them needed a different size paper than we had in the house (I had stocked up on four packages earlier in the year) and the other one needed more mechanical pencil lead. And they both needed it before tomorrow (I'm hearing this at 5 o'clock in the evening, when I need to start our "special" dinner). I started crying – I just couldn't help it. It had all built up and become too much, on a day that I was trying to make special because of our anniversary. Needless to say, I never made the dinner – we ordered take-out.

Finding the Humor

I generally think I'm a pretty humorous person. I can find humor in many situations unless I'm in a bad mood for some reason. I like talking to other moms and while we bitch and complain to each other, we always end up laughing at the ridiculousness of whatever we're discussing. Following are some silly little humorous things that have happened that make me smile or laugh.

- One of our next-door neighbors has grandparents living with them. The older man is a small, thin, but spritely man. I see him sweeping their walkway every now and then. The other day, I took a double-take as I saw him washing the family minivan. He had a pink smock on. Small, little man climbing on the step board to reach the roof of the van, wearing a pink smock - it was a funny visual. I chuckled to myself.

- The electricity in our neighborhood went out abruptly one night for about ½ an hour. I spoke to a neighbor about it the next day. She said she was in the middle of watching the season finale of "Lost" when it hit. You can't help but laugh because – of course!

- My car got hit twice within a month and a half. Both times, the drivers just didn't see me. I drive an SUV for goodness sake – it's a large vehicle! What do I have to do? Paint it fire-engine red?

- Our city's local newspaper had an issue come out the day after our sons' elementary school got locked down because of an armed robbery in our neighborhood. One of the articles featured was about the fact that city officials declared Irvine "America's Safest City" for the fifth consecutive year from the results of an FBI report – the day after the only lockdown in the elementary school's history!

- Our family went to see Zach's first music recital. He played cello for his music class at school. I saved some seats for David and Alex, who joined me later. Before they got there, the principal of the school sat down right beside the last seat I saved. "Good" I thought. Now Alex *(who has spent some time in the principal's office)* will have to sit right next to her during the performance. That will force him to be good!

- Our air conditioner decides to break the evening before the one of the hottest days in August. Of course, I happen to be stuck in the house that whole day because we are getting our ceiling painted, so I can't even run errands in an air-conditioned car or hang out at a nice air-conditioned mall.

- One year I decided to be a room mom in both sons' classes because, although I volunteered regularly in each son's class, I hadn't been a room mom yet and time was running out. There are usually about three or four room moms per class and I was always helping out with parties and going on field trips anyway. Turns out, no other mom offered to be room mom in Alex's class and for some reason, Zach's teacher listed me as the head room mom. So now I was the only room mom in one class and head room mom in the other class – What?! Fortunately, Alex's teacher asked a couple of other moms to help me and all went well that year in both classes and I got to know a few really nice moms better – whew!

Dick and Jane Moment

In an effort to spend some quality time with my older brothers, I would sometimes play softball with them and their friends, with a wiffle ball (thankfully). For some reason, I was always the pitcher and I would inevitably get hit in the head with the ball (now you see why I was thankful it was a wiffle ball). It still hurt, though, a lot! These boys were five and six years older than me! They hit that ball hard! I don't know how much Dick and Jane actually knew about these softball sessions or why I was sometimes coming home bruised. Just trying to be one of the boys.

Supporting Their Strengths

As your children grow older, you start getting a better idea of where their strengths lie. This is one reason why David and I wanted to expose Zach and Alex to many different activities – all types of sports, music, art, cub scouts, science camps, languages, etc. When we see them take an interest in an activity and especially when they're good at it, we try to support it as much as possible. This also helps develop self-esteem and you hope it will help to keep them out of trouble as they enter their teen years.

For example, right now both boys are at an after-school class called Stop Motion Commotion: Animation for Kids. We signed them up for this because it teaches them how to make short videos using legos and action figures. They got interested in this by watching lego videos on YouTube. Now they like to spend time making their own videos and as they get longer and more involved, maybe we'll post them on YouTube also. Who knows, maybe they're two Steven Spielberg's in the making.

As they've gotten older, they've dropped many activities and spend more time on the ones they're really interested in and good at. For example, Zach really loves playing guitar and now takes lessons with the lead guitarist of an Orange County band. Alex, on the other hand, loves messing around on the computer and he's fantastic at solving problems. This coupled with the fact that he's a self-starter and very interested in money (it comes to him easily and seems to grow somehow), has David and me thinking he'll be the next Bill Gates or Steve Jobs.

Priorities

Your priorities change once you become a parent. It's different for everyone, but overall most parents probably find that they care more about what is happening in the world and what the future holds. You also find you care more about your children than you do for yourself – and that's a good thing. You become less selfish and more loving, caring and empathetic.

Becoming a parent definitely made me care more about what was happening in the world and I understand the whole "mama bear" thing. When you become a mother, you become fiercely protective of your children. I had a watchful eye, especially when they were young, and I would stand up for them when they needed it. I also tried to teach them how to protect and stand up for themselves.

Your kids are only young once. Your house can be clean once they leave the nest (remind your husband of this when he comes home from work, sees that the house is a mess and wonders what you did all day). Sometimes you just need to spend time playing with your kids or just listening to them, just hanging out with them. This will help build a stronger bond between you and you want this strong foundation as they enter the tween and teen years. You also want to build an open line of communication.

The Grandparents

As you enter and navigate through motherhood, you may find that your relationship with your parents profoundly changes. You now understand more fully what it must have been like for them. Also, it's fun to see a relationship building between each parent and your children. When your parents take care of your children and enjoy spending time with them, it warms you. I personally felt closer to my parents when I watched how much they loved our children. It helps to ease any strains that have been present in the past – it's a healing force.

Watching my parents with my children makes me look forward to some day becoming a grandmother. I can see how much pleasure you can derive from that relationship and it's good to know that you still get to hand the kids over to their parents. Your responsibilities are less than they were when you were the parent.

I see that I want to routinely be a part of their life from the beginning, so a strong bond is formed. I've learned that I will want to offer to babysit or watch the kids regularly a few times a week and hopefully the parents (my sons and their wives) will jump on it. I've seen that grandparents get to know their grandchildren so much better from being part of their day-to-day life. They learn what their interests are, and this helps them find things to do together. Time and attention are the most important gifts you can give your grandchildren. Sharing their interests is a gift to yourself too, as you get to know them better. This builds a base that will last as they get older, which is very important because they get busier and get their own life as they get older, and if you don't have this strong base in place, your contact with them will be less and less, until you only see them at holidays (gulp!).

Dick and Jane Moment

Jane's mom was eccentric, to say the least. I didn't enjoy going to visit her. First, there was a tree growing in the bedroom I would sleep in. Yes, an actual tree that they built the house around! Then I would hate taking a shower because it always had several spiders in it, I'm sure coming from the tree that was in the house! She seemed to think this was all normal – huh?

Noise

The noise level at our house is almost deafening sometimes. I've often wondered why the cops haven't been called on us (well actually, they have). The boys will get angry at each other and start screaming matches. They'll scream at the top of their lungs because they're mad at each other or because one of them has interrupted the other and the other is trying to be heard. It's hardest when the weather is hot, so we have the windows open to get a breeze. I'm running around trying to calm them down and quiet them. It's especially aggravating when they're upstairs yelling and I'm downstairs trying to make dinner. I can't yell up at them because that just adds to the noise and confusion. So, I have to wait until I can safely walk away from the stove, run up the stairs and quietly tell them to stop yelling. I'm so mad at this point, I'm fuming and I'm thinking under my breath, "just shut-up!"

Now don't let me give you the false impression that I don't ever blow my top and start yelling back, because I'm just not that virtuous. I'm sure there are times when the middle-aged single lady next door who's never had kids thinks I'm an awful mother, but she just doesn't get it. At least I know our home is not the only one with loud, screaming children. A few of my mom friends have admitted that their children scream like banshees sometimes and they have to scream also to be heard. We laugh about it and it makes us feel better, because it's so embarrassing while it's happening.

Apart from the yelling, our boys just seem to like a lot of noise. Seems they've gotten used to it … hmm… For example, they have the TV and video games on really loud. It seems that David and I are always asking them to turn down the volume. We've even wondered about their hearing, but we've gotten both of their hearing checked a myriad of times and everything's fine. Really, doctor, really?? Are you SURE?

When Your Kids Are Driving You Crazy ('Cause Sometimes They Will)

Well you can tell I'm having one of those days because if I'm writing a chapter on this, I must be. Right now, my oldest son is in his bedroom doing his homework because he went absolutely ballistic on me when I told him he needed to stop playing with legos and start on homework. Mind you, we had already agreed that he would begin homework at 3:00 and I set the timer, so he and his brother would know when it was time to stop playing. After the timer went off and I threatened taking some money from their wallets (an effective form of discipline in our household), his younger brother started doing homework, while he started yelling and asking for more time. He did not do this in a polite manner, but in a demanding manner. After he kept getting money taken away from him, I had had enough and sent him to his room. I'm exhausted. I don't know the physical process of what happens to my body in this situation, but it just exhausts me. It must be the amount of stress hormones coursing through my veins. Now I'm in a bad mood and there's a dark cloud over the rest of this afternoon. I was looking forward to taking the boys to the pool after homework, but now I really don't feel like going. I feel like lying on the sofa and just retreating.

When the kids are yelling and really acting up, I'm tempted to take out a video camera and tape them, so I can play it back to them when they're grown up to prove how difficult they were at times. Come to think of it, maybe I will do it one of these times and show it to them a day or so later, once everything has calmed down and become a distant memory. That way they can see how irrational their behavior was. I don't know if they would actually learn from this or if it would just embarrass them or get them angry or upset again. I really may try it one of these times to find out.

Of course, when they get like this everything is my fault. It's my fault that they are so angry and upset that they're yelling and can't calm down. It's my fault that I'm making them do what they're supposed to instead of what they want to, even when they agreed to it beforehand. It's somehow my fault that they have so much homework in the first place. Because it's my fault that they even have to go to school! I'll just have to go read this section in my book when they're grown and I'm an empty-nester and am missing them – just to remind myself that every day was not all sunshine and roses with a cherry on top.

Under Pressure

Stress is a word we all know very well as parents. It starts from the moment you find out you're pregnant. You're worried about your baby's health, your health, your finances with raising a child to adulthood, the world the baby is coming into, the things you need to buy to get ready for the baby's arrival, etc. etc. When the baby is a newborn, the stress comes mostly from tending to this little person's constant needs. A newborn baby is a feeding, peeing, pooping, sleeping, crying machine and you are constantly trying to assess what he/she needs. The sleeping portion never lasts long enough, and the stress comes not only from feeling overwhelmed from all these needs and demands but also from the fact that you are severely sleep-deprived.

As the children get older, the stress never goes away, it just changes forms – just like energy. If you remember from science class, energy is never created nor destroyed, it just changes forms. Anyway, once your baby becomes mobile, you must constantly monitor where your baby is. I actually liked it when my boys went to walking from crawling because I could see them better and thus it was easier to keep track of them. Also, I always wanted the floor and carpet to be clean when they were crawling because babies are notorious for picking up things from the floor and putting it into their mouths – yuck! I was adamant that people remove their shoes when they walked into our house.

When they're toddlers, they need you to help entertain them. They just don't stay on an activity for very long. At least that was my experience. I listened longingly to some mothers as they described their little girl sitting quietly in her room coloring for over an hour. Definitely not my experience. Also, wherever you take them you must be ever-vigilant. You have to be right behind them at the park, so they don't fall off the ladders or monkey bars and you have to get into the pool with them and be right there, even if they have a life vest or floaties, so they don't accidentally slip under the water.

Once they start school, the stress comes from social issues - school work, homework and eventually their growing independence. You worry about if they have enough friends, who their friends are, when difficulties arise in their friendships, if they're meeting grade-level expectations in their schoolwork, whether they're exceeding these expectations, how well they're doing their homework, fighting with them about doing their homework, when they can walk alone to a neighbor's house or to school, when to hang back and when to step in. All of this gets pretty exhausting. I can't even imagine what the stress will be like when they are driving or dating – yikes! I better get myself into a meditation routine by then – Ommm!

Live in the Moment (well … try)

Zach is going into middle school soon. Realizing how much time has passed while it has seemed like a relatively short time reminds me again and again to try as much as possible to live in the moment. Mind you, there are times when I don't want to live in the moment, I just want it to go by as soon as possible because the kids are fighting or driving me crazy or I'm stressed or exhausted or whatever. But I really do try to focus on the fact that this is all just a drop in the bucket of time and at some point, there will be an empty nest and I will miss all of this. So at least if I try to drink it all in wholeheartedly right now, I can be comforted by the fact that I fully experienced each day, each moment.

I remember my mom saying, "the days are long but the years are short". I really hated when she said this because it was always when I was most frustrated, angry and exhausted. She was trying to make me feel better by putting things into perspective for me (I guess). But it just pissed me off more because I didn't feel sentimental at the time. Worse, it would make me feel guilty for feeling whatever I was at the time because I knew she was right. However, when she wasn't around I would catch myself thinking about this during trying moments. So, I did try to put things into perspective myself and realize that I will miss all this someday.

Now as the boys are getting older, I really try to live in the moment because I'm much more acutely aware of time slipping away and sometimes, it makes me really sad. I love watching the individuals they are becoming and as they get older, our relationship progresses, but I also miss the little boys they were and being able to kiss them and hug them without them cringing or running away (sigh).

Wabi Sabi

Wabi Sabi, you say, what is that? It's a term that originated in Japan to explain the imperfections of life and to not only explain them, but to make peace with them. In fact, some artists will leave cracks or imperfections in their work to honor the idea of Wabi Sabi. It's a useful way of thought in life to not always strive for perfection but to accept and appreciate the imperfect, ruggedness of everyday life. It is through this imperfection that we can grow and learn and decipher what is most meaningful in our lives. It's the idea that if you see a crack in something, that's OK – that's how the light gets in. When you are a parent, you start to realize that there's a lot of Wabi Sabi in your life and you can either make peace with it or let it drive you crazy. Here are some of the Wabi Sabi things in our life.

Our carpet. Our carpet is always in need of cleaning. But there are always just too many things stuffed around our house to get a carpet cleaner to come in. Then we got a cat who would go into our yard, then come in to throw up on our carpet – why oh why wouldn't she throw up outside? Then we were looking for a puppy. Well who's foolhardy enough to clean carpets before getting a puppy? So we had to look at it in a Wabi Sabi kind of way. It was a livable and lived through carpet. We will clean it when things calm down (what, in 20 years?)

Also, my house in general has a Wabi Sabi quality. At any given moment, there are all sorts of different toys, cards, school supplies, clothes strewn all over the floors, tables, counters and any other surfaces. I try to keep up with them, really, I do. But I swear, 30 minutes after I've cleaned, you can look around and not notice that I have accomplished anything. I get our boys to do some chores but by the next day, everything is back to – well, Wabi Sabi. So, I get tired and periodically, I give up. I give in to the Wabi Sabiness of it all and throw up my hands, realizing that when there are no longer children living in the house, the house will be much more organized and clean. In the meantime ….

My body. I'm constantly trying to drop about 10 pounds (or more). I go walking for 45 minutes, then on alternate days, I get on my exercise bike for 50 minutes. I do usually get a good amount of exercise. But it just doesn't seem to work enough, and things always seem to get in the way of my schedule which forces me to skip working out or to cut it short. Beyond the weight, it seems as if my feet could always use a pedicure and my fingernails need to be clipped, filed and painted. But of course, there never seems to be enough time for that and it generally falls by the wayside. Sometimes I'll get lucky and find enough time to get a pedicure (my one real extravagance) and I'll keep it up for a couple of months over the summer. It's June now, though, and I haven't been able to get a pedicure yet. Oh well, Wabi Sabi feet.

My to-do list. There is always so much to do that I never feel like I catch up. I do like to make lists to keep up with it all and make sure I don't forget anything. That also helps me in the middle of the night to not start thinking about everything because I'm afraid I'll forget something. I find I'm always running around trying to take care of the thing that has the first deadline. It's not always the most important thing, but the most urgent. I have to sometimes just stop and take a breath and realize to try to live in the moment instead of having events just pass me by in a blur.

The Nitty Gritty

Clutter

It never stops! I just spent yesterday, all day, sorting through the outdated toys in our office/playroom. This is a process that I do fairly regularly and it's amazing how quickly it will start to build up again. I was breaking a sweat for most of the day as I was putting toys, games and books into various bags (some for charity and some to throw away) and taking trash bag after trash bag to our trash bin in the garage. Our bin is now overflowing – it's a good thing it's trash day tomorrow. I now have to haul all the other bags to a local charity. It does make me feel good to give these to children who will have more use for them and really appreciate them.

Do you know how many bags I have stashed outside of the room? 24 – twenty-four!! And some items are too big to put in bags. As I mentioned before, I do this on a fairly regular basis. I don't usually have this much stuff, but there is a charity that comes to our neighborhood about once a month and I usually have about five bags to give them every couple of months. I just got fed up yesterday. Alex's birthday is coming up and we'll have the family over to celebrate his birthday (he'll have a separate party with his friends). We want to get the carpets cleaned but there's just too much stuff on the ground to even have a carpet cleaning service come.

I clean up clutter or at least throw some stuff away and pile the leftovers in neat, orderly piles and it seems like a day later, everything's piling up and spreading out again. And forget about it when friends come over. There's stuff all over the place then. I ask and nag my children to put their things away, but it just gets stuffed to the side or stashed under the bed or sofas. Do other mothers feel this way? I've heard distant stories of some mothers telling their children to clean up and they do. I even know one mother who's place always looks orderly. I seriously don't know how she does it. She says she just keeps at it each day (I try to!) But she also says – get this – that she actually likes cleaning! In fact, her husband admits that she's a bit of a nut about it. Also, she has two boys, like I do, but they are about six years apart. My sons are about a year and a half apart and they seem to feed on each other's frenzy. So, I think that has something to do with it as well. Of course, I know I'm rationalizing, but it makes me feel better.

One of the times during the year that increases clutter is the end of the school year. Your children proudly walk in with their work throughout the year. Their backpacks are stuffed with used school supplies and projects, then they come home with piles of artwork, writing, math, different notebooks, folders and used books. I always figure out we'll sort it out in a day or two, but weeks later, I seem to keep walking by the piles. Of course, you want to keep most of their work as keepsakes, but really, you can't keep everything – every year.

One thing I started to do is to have storage bins under our bed. I have one for Zach and one for Alex. I will store their best artwork and school work in there. I have separate ones for preschool, kindergarten and now 1st through whichever grade I can squeeze in. The preschool and kindergarten ones are now stored in our garage. If a piece of work is too large to store here, I might store it separately or take a couple of pictures of it before we dispose of it. This way we always have a memory of it. With the boys' school supplies, I try to go through and see which ones we can reuse for the next year or keep for use at home. I sometimes keep old school books or try to think of someone with a younger child who might find it useful.

When the Kids Are Home

When the kids are home, say for vacation or they're sick, I seem to get nothing done. Moreover, it seems as if I'm doing the same things throughout the day – making food and cleaning up (putting food away, washing dishes, wiping counters, wiping the table). In between I might try to do laundry, make some phone calls, pay some bills. But I will inevitably get interrupted or distracted, which makes it very difficult to actually finish these duties. As I'm writing this section, both boys are home sick from school and I have been making food, cleaning up (over and over), responding to desperate calls for me (they want a snack – again), stopping to go downstairs to try to find a DVD, taking temperatures, fetching water – you get the picture. I'm really not making this up. "Mom!" "Yesss". I try not to sound irritated.

So, my husband will come home at the end of the day and wonder why the living room looks the way it does, as I have been home all day. What he doesn't realize it that the living room looks that way because the children have been home all day. I pick up after them, because I feel bad – they're sick. Twenty minutes later, it looks like I've done nothing! David will wonder why I seem a bit frazzled and why I'm so tired. He's had a long, grueling day at work and a hellish commute. It doesn't seem fair for me to complain, but I do try to get him to understand that I am doing work at home. And to be fair, he is pretty good about understanding it. He's had times when he's taken care of the boys and he gets a taste of it on weekends, when we're all home.

Then there are breaks and Summer, when the kids are home for extended periods. Sometimes these breaks are broken up, if you will, by vacations or half-day camps. But sometimes, I just have to try to keep them occupied. Zach and Alex happen to go to a year-round school, so they get evenly spaced breaks throughout the year – 3 weeks during the Fall, 3 weeks in Winter, 3 weeks for Spring break and usually about 5 weeks for Summer.

I'm just finishing a 3-week Spring break right now and generally it went well, although I didn't completely finish those things I wanted to do. Before the break, I thought about sitting down with the boys and listing things we wanted to do. They never seemed interested in making that list, so I ended up doing it in my head. I used the time to also get appointments out of the way for them – doctors, dentists, hair cuts, etc. I'm chagrined to say we never made it to the library – we have two more days. We didn't get out and exercise as much as I had hoped. But we did make a trip to downtown L.A. one day to visit David at his office and have lunch with him. Afterwards, I drove them to Hollywood and we walked around. They were excited because they always wanted to see Hollywood, having seen it in different movies and TV shows. We did have lunch one day with their grandparents and had their friends over. We slept in and stayed up late. We went to our neighborhood pool at night and pretended we were on vacation.

So all in all, it was a pretty good break although they did have times when they were bored but didn't like any of my suggestions to go out and do things. Of course, I didn't get much done. I barely got to work on this book, the house was perpetually messy although I was picking up and cleaning each day and I seriously fell back on my exercising, particularly walking, and now feel bloated and keep looking for fatter clothes among the fat clothes in my closet.

"Mom, What's Sex?"

Well first, let me start by saying that David and I listened to the experts and used the correct anatomical names for the body parts dealing with sex. Zach and Alex knew from a young age that they had penises and that girls and women have vaginas. We made this no big deal, hoping that questions about sex down the road would be easier.

As they questioned us about how to make babies, I would try to gauge how much information they really wanted to know. When they were young, we explained that babies grew in their mom's tummy. They seemed to be fine with that information and would move on to something else. Recently, my older son asked, "what's sex?" Instinctively, I felt he didn't want a lengthy description about how to make a baby, he just wanted to know what that word meant. So, I told him that sex is how a mom and a dad make a baby. He made a face, said "yuck" and moved on. When they've asked me specific questions, I've started to answer them with broad information, trying to figure out how specific I should get. At this point, they've always said "OK, OK" so I know enough is enough and their satisfied for now. I always want the boys to feel that they can talk to us about sex and ask us any questions. I do think they will spend more time going to their father.

In 5th grade at our school, they have a "Guys Stuff" evening for dads and sons and a mother-daughter tea to explain some of the physical and emotional changes that accompany puberty. They don't go into sex education per se, but do touch on the changes that happen during puberty and how their bodies are transitioning into adulthood. During "Guy Stuff", they also talked about personal hygiene issues and increased responsibilities now that they're beginning to move into manhood. I do think as parents that while we are teaching our children the fundamentals of sex and answering their questions, it's important to impart our values to them. We need to put this information into the context of love, relationships and responsibility. We need to teach them what our expectations are, while at the same time keeping the lines of communication open. I believe in teaching our children the facts about birth control and STDs so they have all the information they need as they enter the increasingly responsible world of adulthood.

“Mom, What’s the ‘F’ Word?”

Are you kidding me? At some point your children are going to get more familiar with bad words. It starts when they’re young when they innocently say a bad word that they heard you or your husband slip out. If you react too strongly, they think it’s funny or just realize that they have power to get a reaction out of you. So, you calmly let them know that it is not OK to say this word. They look at you with doe eyes and say that they were just repeating what they heard you or daddy say. You embarrassingly say that the word was an accident and that none of you should be saying it.

When they get older, they start to hear these words on TV, on the radio, through friends and through older kids at school. They get the idea that certain words are taboo, especially at school. They start to wonder what these words mean and the next thing you know, they’re asking you what the “F” word means. You tell them that it’s just bad and people don’t like hearing it. My boys persisted so I told them people sometimes use it when they’re really angry. If they keep going, I finally just say that I can’t explain it because they wouldn’t understand it yet so give it a rest. Eventually they move on to something else once they realize I’m not going to discuss it anymore.

Sleep

I remember David's aunt telling me that you never have good sleep after you have kids. She was in her 70's when she told me this. Her husband and she had stopped off in California on their way back to Wisconsin from a trip they just took to Australia. They had a wonderful time, but she never gets a full night of sleep without waking up, even on vacation. That spooked me, but it does seem to be true. To be completely fair, though, I do think it also has something to with age, for men as well as women. It's just that, having children disrupts your sleep so profoundly and routinely that this lack of sleep probably happens much earlier than it normally would.

In the beginning when you bring your new baby home, he needs to eat every couple of hours. So, you are constantly being awakened, even if you're not the person feeding him. I remember that after feeding my sons, I tried to drift off to sleep as soon as possible because I would only have about 1 ½ hours to sleep until the next feeding. If I stayed awake, I may only have one hour. So, I desperately willed myself to sleep. I sometimes would feel so groggy during the day, it was hard to function. David would feed the boys a bottle once in the middle of the night so I could get some more sleep, bless him. We ended up getting on a schedule where each baby would eat at 12 midnight, 2am, then 5am. The 5am feeding for some reason *killed* me. I would wake up with a raging headache that just wouldn't go away. Then I would have a hard time going back to sleep. So, David took over that feeding and things went smoothly. You learn to adjust with broken-up sleep.

When the boys each slept through the night (midnight to 6am), it was cause for celebration. We could actually get almost six hours of uninterrupted sleep if we fell asleep quickly after the midnight feeding. Then they got older and started sleeping for a longer period of time and life finally got back into a more normal routine. The next big milestone in their lives which interrupted the sleep schedule was moving from the crib to a "big kid" bed. This allowed them to easily get out of bed, which they learned to do quickly and would do often. They would keep getting out of bed once you put them down for a variety of excuses, like needing a glass of water, having to go to the bathroom or hearing something. They also learned how easy it was to come to our bed in the middle of the night when they woke up. This was an extremely frustrating period of time until we finally worked through this stage.

A few techniques that helped us were we would close their bedroom door if they came out too often. They hated having the door closed so this was an effective strategy. Also, we would let them sometimes sleep with us on the weekends if they stayed in their beds during the week. Once our boys shared a room, a lot of that behavior stopped because they didn't get scared as much since they had each other. They would visit for awhile before they fell asleep, although sometimes we had to stop them from talking too long.

Moms are always tired – dads are too. Here are some tricks I've used to keep my energy up when I'm feeling sluggish.

- Cat nap – even just a quick doze of 15-20 minutes can give you a little extra energy when you most need it. The funny thing is that when my sons were young, they used to hate to see me lying down with closed eyes. They always used to come over and say, "don't go to sleep". So, I would put on a 30-minute video and close my eyes while they were busy watching that.

- Caffeine – of course. I'll have some green tea after lunch. This gives me a little caffeine, but not as much as coffee, which I have in the morning. I can't have any caffeine after about 2 PM or it interferes with my sleep at night.

- Go for a walk. I'll try to walk outside for a bit even if it's just going to the mailbox. Being outside wakes you up a bit along with the movement of walking.

- Light – if I'm trying to wake up in the morning, I'll open all drapes and blinds. The light helps stimulate your mind by letting it know it's time to wake up. If it's in the middle of the day, I try to go outside even for a couple of minutes to get some outdoor light.

- Cold water – splash some on your face, like when you're washing your face first thing in the morning, which is generally the only time I do this because later in the day it would interfere with my makeup.

Communication

It's always been important to David and I that we try to establish an open line of communication with Zach and Alex. We've always encouraged them to ask us questions and let us know what's on their minds no matter what. We also tried to encourage them to always tell us the truth by letting them know that if they tell us the truth about something bad they did, they won't get into as much trouble. However, if we found out they had lied to us and we told them we would usually eventually find out, they would be in even more trouble – first for the infraction and second for the lying.

We also realize that for communication to be effective, it needs to be a two-way street. By that, I mean we have to listen as much as, preferably more than, we talk. We need to ask the boys open-ended questions and make time to have opportunities where conversations can naturally occur. One routine time we have to discuss things is dinner. We make a point to all sit down whenever possible and discuss the day's events. Another time that David uses mostly is right before bed. Zach and Alex are in bed and the lights are out and David will have a discussion with them. They love this and look forward to this routine. They can talk about anything they want. We even also use weekday breakfasts as a time to touch base with them before the day starts (on the weekends, we let them eat breakfast while watching the TV – a no-no, I know, but sometimes you need to indulge them.)

Additionally, a couple of time periods I take advantage of are while I'm walking them to school and after they come home from school. They tend to open up during these times because their attention isn't being taken away elsewhere. As they've gotten older and walk to and from school by themselves, I have to find other opportunities to get them to open up. Sometimes it's easier to get them to talk while you're in the car. It must have something to do with not having to have direct eye contact that helps them to open up more.

So far, we have been very pleased with the amount of information they've shared with us. They give us details about what happens at school and come and talk to us when something is bothering them. This way, we're able to advise and guide them. We try to keep encouraging this while they are still young because we realize that as they get older, this will naturally diminish, but we're trying to keep the door open as long and as wide as possible.

Money Grows on Trees (Oh Really?)

During the recession of 2008-2009, things became hard financially for our family, as well as many others. David's office closed, and he was looking for another advertising job right when jobs were worse than scarce, they were essentially non-existent. Advertising is one of the first industries to suffer during a recession and one of the last to rebound. He finally found a job though it was not on par at all in terms of quality of work or pay.

During this time, I tried to decrease our expenses as much as possible and was forced out of necessity to be very creative in doing this. To our surprise, it wasn't always as painful as we would have anticipated. The first thing to go was that we didn't eat out as often. Then when we did eat out we would go to cheaper places and utilize coupons. Also, I scrutinized how much we were spending on groceries and slashed that quite a bit. I had always clipped coupons but now I did it with a fervor, bought items on sale and planned the menu for the week based on this, shopped around for the best deal to a certain extent (as long as I wasn't using too much gas driving around) and cooked almost everything from scratch. It's amazing how much you can save just by not buying convenience items as much. We still ate really well and this didn't really cut our quality of life. It was more work for me, but I ended up liking the taste of everything from scratch better and liked the idea that it was healthier because I had control of what I was putting in our meals.

When we had to get really strict with our budget, we explained to our boys that we had to be careful with our money, like many other families had to. We explained that dad's new job didn't pay as much as the old job and that the economy was tough and most families were having to tighten their belts so they would realize that we were not alone in this. We explained the concept that there are always people who are better off than you and people that are worse off than you, so just do your best with what you have instead of comparing yourself to others.

We also got more creative when it came to holidays and vacations. For example, on Father's Day (and Mother's Day), we traditionally went to an outdoor patio area on the bar side of a restaurant on the San Clemente pier. We started this tradition when the boys were younger because it was a casual atmosphere outdoors and it didn't matter so much if the boys were loud – there was always a lot of activity and noise going on. Most people clamored to get an ocean view, but we would go to the back, which was near the railroad tracks. The trains coming and going helped entertain the boys and keep them occupied.

For Father's Day in 2009, we still wanted to spend some time at the beach without spending a lot of money. So, we decided to go to a beautiful beach that has a big grassy hill where you can play catch, fly kites, roll down the hill, etc. We used to come here with the boys so they could run around the grass and then go down and frolic in the beach. David and I also would sometimes come here with a picnic by ourselves to have a romantic time watching the sun set over the water. We decided to have a picnic and just enjoy the view and let the boys run around. This way we could have fun without spending much money. Everyone had a great time. David and the boys played catch and wrestled in the grass. Then we watched the sun set and then we went down to the beach so the boys could body surf until it got too dark. This ended up being one of our best and most memorable Father's Day because it was more active and involving than just sitting at a restaurant.

To teach them about money in a concrete way they could directly relate to, we gave them each a weekly allowance. We wanted to teach them about working for money and how to budget. This showed them that if they wanted more money because they were saving up for a special item, they had to think of jobs to do to make more. This also taught them how to save. At first, they would use up their money fairly quickly. Then when they wanted something and didn't have the money for it, we explained why it was important to save money and not just spend it impulsively right away. We would figure out, based on the item's price, how long it would take them to save up for it. It was a great way to teach them about delayed gratification. A bonus feature was this also made them wait to get the desired item and sometimes, they would figure out that it wasn't worth the cost – this taught them the concept of value.

Dick and Jane Moment

Dick was quite frugal. When I was 12 years old and living with him and my brothers after my parents' divorce, if I wanted to buy clothes, I needed to pay for them myself. I think he was trying to teach me responsibility and the value of a dollar, but … I was 12 years old and only making money by baby-sitting. Needless to say, I was not the best-dressed girl in the neighborhood.

Pets

If you don't already have a pet, invariably your children will want one and beg for one at some point. David and I held out as long as possible but as Zach and Alex got older, we realized it was going to be inevitable that they would have a pet. We just started feeling too bad about keeping them from having this experience since we both grew up with dogs, cats or both.

We decided to start small to teach them about taking care of pets. Our first pets were hermit crabs. Zach had a friend who had a couple of them and the amount of care they needed seemed reasonable and they were cute enough. Both boys had a hermit crab. Our crabs didn't last very long. I think we got them too big and therefore too old in the first place. We had a hard time finding large enough shells for them as they grew. Zach's died first and he was very sad. We put him in a shoe box, buried him in our backyard and had a little ceremony for him. When Alex's crab died, he wasn't bothered much, and we just threw him away (such a sentimental chap.) After a few more attempts at more crabs, the boys weren't intrigued by them so much any more.

Then Alex went to a birthday party and the gift given to all the attendees was a goldfish (great!). Well, we had to go straight to the pet store to get a small aquarium for the fish and to get one for Zach. Several fish later, the boys stopped being intrigued with these creatures as well. I learned that unless you have a nice, big filtered aquarium, fish can be very disgusting.

Finally, we decided we would get a cat. The boys picked out Zoey at an adoption day at a local pet store. She was warm and furry and would sleep with the boys and not take too much work. The hardest part was dealing with her litter box. The boys learned to feed her and this became part of their chores. Zoey's personality wasn't real cuddly, though. She preferred to be on her own and would only come to you if she felt like it. You could pet her, but she didn't like to be held. So, the boys kept being interested in other pets even though they did love Zoey.

For Zach's 10th birthday he decided he wanted something called a bearded dragon. It's a very popular reptile and we really thought about getting it for Zach. Then we found out about all the work involved. This creature needs about a 40 lb. tank with two different heating bulbs, two temperature gauges, a rock to bask on and stuff at the bottom of the tank. They are omnivores and need to eat meat, vegetables and fruit. So once a day you give them some vegetables and fruit, but no lettuce or citrus fruits. When they're young you feed them live crickets twice a day. They can eat 30-60 crickets at each feeding! Every other day you need to dust the crickets with calcium powder. You can also feed them mealworms, cockroaches, and other bugs (yuck!)

They need to be given a bath once a week to keep them hydrated since they usually won't drink water from a water dish. You also need to spray them in their tank if they're not drinking water, but you have to be careful because you don't want to get the tank too humid. After you bathe them, you have to disinfect the bathtub and they will usually defecate in the water (nice!). Of course, you also have to wash your hands after handling them so they don't transmit salmonella to you. Well, after learning about all of this, David and I agreed that taking care of a dog would be a lot less hassle and time-consuming.

So along came Lucky. We took months looking for the right dog for our family. We researched the best breed for our family and went to numerous pet adoption events. We saw Lucky at a large adoption event at our local animal shelter. He was about 8 weeks old and was the only puppy left from his litter, even his mom had been adopted. He was sleeping and he was so cute! The boys were immediately drawn to him and wanted him. We picked him up and held him and then David took the boys around to look at all the other dogs to make sure he was the one we wanted. I stayed and held Lucky so someone wouldn't get him while they were gone. The boys made up their mind and Lucky became ours.

He was white and looked like he might have some Lab in him. The boys named him Lucky because we stopped at Petco to get him some items on the way home. As we were holding him in line, a big dog behind us barked and lunged at him. The boys said he was lucky that day because the big dog didn't get him and we were lucky to get him. Hence, his name was born. As he's grown it's become apparent that there is no Lab in his mix. He now seems to have a mix of Terrier, Chihuahua and Daschund – three breeds that David didn't want in a dog (LOL).

He's become a great addition to our family and is really a wonderful dog. He has a great temperament, obeys us and protects us. When he barks, he sounds much bigger than he is (he's about 30 lbs.) People are always surprised when we open the door. They are apprehensive and look ahead to see the big dog that's been barking, then are surprised when they have to look down to see him. As David now says, he may not have been the type of dog we originally wanted, but he's the dog we needed.

Dick and Jane Moment

All our pets had human names. We had a cat named Megan. Then we had Saint Bernard dogs named Timothy, Hannah, Sean and Rory. Our friends thought this was funny and a bit odd. With respect to Timothy, he was big enough (and patient enough) for me to ride him like a horse (I kid you not) when I was a little girl. I had my own version of my own little "pony".

Video Games/Technology

Everybody seems to complain about kids playing video games or using digital devices too much. Sure, there needs to be limits, but let me play devil's advocate for a minute and tell my reasons why video games and digital devices can be a positive leisure activity once these limits are in place.

First, I'll discuss video games. These games strengthen hand-eye coordination and are an active leisure form, unlike watching TV. The kids have to think and act quickly in these games and they can play with multiple partners or just themselves. Also, most, if not all, of the kids at school play various video games. It's part of the kids' culture. If your kids don't play, they aren't able to relate to an important aspect of other kids' play activities. Of course, you have to control which video games your child plays. Some of them do get violent so you need to be aware of the rating system to make sure you're comfortable with the games their playing.

As for technology, kids will need to learn how to navigate this for the rest of their lives. Technology is part of the curriculum at our sons' schools. Children need to know how to operate basic programs. This will always help them in their future jobs. It's also important that they learn to navigate the internet. Of course, they need to learn internet safety. They need to be taught not to give any personal information over the internet including their name, address, phone number, parents' names and school name/location. They also need to be taught that anything they put on the internet can be there forever.

So, they need to be taught to be very careful, especially with social networking sites. They also need to be warned in an age-appropriate manner of the risks of predators and that this is why it is so important not to give out personal information; not everyone is who they say they are. A 40-year old man can easily pretend to be a 13-year old girl in cyberspace. But once they grasp proper use of the internet, social sites, e-mail and texting, they become valuable tools in getting information, communicating and building connections. It is the wave of the future, so our kids need to be interacting with it, front and center, whether we like it or not.

Discipline

The American Heritage Dictionary defines discipline as "training expected to produce a specific character or pattern of behavior." The biggest component of discipline is to try to teach your children how to behave properly. The goal is for them to internalize these lessons so they will follow them even when you aren't around and for them to eventually live a successful life on their own. So, discipline is different from just simple punishment in that we want to positively reinforce desired behaviors instead of just focusing on the negative ones. However, as any parent knows, punishment is a useful learning tool. When the kids just aren't listening or obeying you, punishment gets their attention.

I try to use positive reinforcement as often as possible with my sons but unfortunately see myself having to use punishment or the threat of it more often than I would like. One of the most effective punishments I've used with my children and have seen other parents utilize is to take something favorable away – a favorite object, a privilege, a fun event, etc. Examples of this are to take away a favorite toy, TV time, or being able to go to a friend's house or some other event they were looking forward to. One of our sons is very money-oriented and they both get an allowance each week and do chores to earn it. One of the most effective strategies we have found for both of them is to threaten to take away some of that allowance. Then they really feel it when they don't get their normal amount. I usually wouldn't take away a playdate for my children because I didn't feel that was fair to the other child.

I've had other mother's do this and I'm just not a big fan of that. I've then had to deal with my son's disappointment and they didn't do anything wrong.

Another way I use discipline is that the boys can get what they want by giving me what I want. For example, we have our traditional Friday night popcorn night where I spread out a sheet on the living room floor and we all eat popcorn and watch a movie or TV. But this will not happen if the living room is messy. So, Zach and Alex have to straighten up the living room beforehand. Now I found that they used to just shove a lot of stuff under our sofas and figure it was cleaned up because it looked good. I had to teach them that they actually had to clean it up and put things away where they belong. I realized that they may need me to spell out the steps to do it. So, I would tell them to pick up anything that just needed to be thrown away. Then pick up anything that could be put in recycling. Then pick up all the stray legos and put them in the lego box. Finally, look around and anything else on the ground needed to be picked up and put in its proper place and that may mean, yes, having to take it upstairs. The added bonus to this is that it actually teaches them to clean up after themselves, so their future wives won't hate me.

One thing I've learned is not to quickly judge another parent disciplining or punishing their child unless there is obvious abuse. You just don't know the full story or history of what is going on. I feel I've been on each side of being judged for being too lenient and too hard with discipline. But these people do not see the history of how my husband and I deal with each child and if I seem too lenient, the person doesn't see that really, I've learned to pick my battles. If you are constantly "on" your child, they tend to tune you out and all communication and punishment seems to become less effective.

On those instances where I might seem harsh, the person doesn't realize that this is a chosen battle. This might be an issue we've been working on for awhile that my child knows is non-negotiable. So, I'm going to come down hard on him to remind him that he can't get away with it and that it is not acceptable behavior. I've seen other mothers in these situations, too, and I know it isn't always exactly as it looks to the observer because I know these mothers, their children and their individual circumstances. There are also physical, developmental or behavioral issues that may make some children more difficult to discipline than others, such as autism or ADHD. You just have to assume that you don't know the whole situation.

Driving Around

I always used to hear mothers complain about all the driving around they have to do, shuttling their children from one activity to another. For me, driving the children around is not the issue. I don't mind driving, in fact I find it rather pleasurable. The hard part is when they have overlapping practices, games or classes and trying to coordinate everything. It gets easier as they get older because you can drop them off. For games, you want to be there to watch. There have been many times when David and I had to take one child to his game while the other went to the other child's, so they each had at least one parent present. Sometimes you get lucky enough to be able to find another mom to carpool with, but my experience is that it doesn't happen often. We're either coming from different areas or the timing doesn't match up.

Another hard part of all the practices, games, classes, etc., is getting the kids to be ready to leave on time. This seems to always be a taxing issue. If it's after school, I'm trying to give them a snack and get them to do as much homework as possible before they have to get changed and get out the door. I'm also usually trying to prep dinner as much as possible because I won't have much time to cook it by the time we get back home. If it's on the weekend, they get busy with other activities at home like playing with legos, video games or watching TV. It's so hard to get them to stop and focus on getting ready. If it's early in the morning on a Saturday or Sunday, they complain about having to get up early on a non-school day. I commiserate with them on this one, but you just have to bite the bullet sometimes.

Part of what makes me not dislike driving around is that I absolutely love my car – LOVE it! It's not fancy, but it's exactly what I need and makes my life easier. It's an SUV and we bought it to have enough space as the boys got older. I do feel guilty about gas mileage, but this vehicle actually does pretty well for an SUV. Also, I try to be strategic in how I drive. I bundle errands together so I'm on one side of the town one day and the other another day. That way I minimize how much I'm driving. This car is great for my shopping trips – I fill up the back every week. It's also fantastic for not only transporting my sons and their gear, but their friends as well. This was one of the reasons we got it – our previous vehicle didn't have enough seats for each child to bring a friend in the car. Where this car really shines, though is on trips, especially skiing trips. We can pack this bad boy with all our stuff and believe me we do.

This vehicle has gotten us through many snow storms without us even needing to install chains, although we always carry them in case. In fact, this car got us down the mountain in the worst storm David and I have ever seen, and David grew up in Wisconsin. It was complete white-out conditions and you couldn't see the road. We had to inch along, and David and I had to keep getting out of the car to scratch off the ice and snow that continually accumulated on the windshield. I was really scared and couldn't believe they hadn't closed the road! Hours later, when we finally made it down the mountain, we found out they had closed the road in both directions about half an hour after we started down the mountain. That SUV got us down safely while we saw numerous cars stranded on the sides.

After that experience, I'm going to keep my vehicle as long as it will keep running. And from now on, if it looks like there's even a chance of hitting a snowstorm going up or down the mountain, we're going to wait, even if we have to spend an extra night on the mountain (bummer – can't make it to work or school because we got caught in a snowstorm).

When Your Child Gets Sick

When your child gets sick, your mothering impulses turn on in full gear. You want to tuck him into bed and make him feel more comfortable. You try to feed him chicken soup, herbal tea, lots of water, anything to try to make him feel better fast. You try to keep him as comfortable as possible and have him sleep as much as possible to help his body fight the illness. You need to decide if it's something to make a doctor's appointment about or just wait it out. When your child complains of vague symptoms just before school, it's sometimes hard to decipher if he's really sick or just doesn't want to go to school for some reason. If he doesn't have a fever or any obvious symptoms, it's hard to know. When that's been the case, I've told my child that he can't spend the day watching TV or playing video games. He needs to spend most of the day in his bed and when he feels good enough, he needs to read. As my boys have gotten older, I've also e-mailed the teachers to make sure they're keeping on top of schoolwork. I'll sometimes stop at school to pick up work or try to find a friend willing to deliver it. So, I try to make sure that it doesn't seem like too much of a break, if they're trying to use it just as an excuse.

Of course, when one child gets sick, you have to watch the whole family because we can all start dropping like dominoes. Once we had children, David and I started getting the flu shot each year because we experienced how completely awful it can be to be feeling absolutely sick and still having to care for your children. You can be feeling that you can't get off the couch, but your children are hungry and they need you to prepare them some food.

Alex somehow has the immune system of a … I don't know what – they need to study him because he barely ever gets sick and when he does, it doesn't last. For example, when he was around six, he once got a fever of 105º. We gave him some child's Tylenol and he was back to normal in about half an hour, never acting sick again. David and I were amazed! A couple of years earlier, his brother had a temperature that high and we ended up in the emergency room with him. It took him a couple of days to completely return to normal.

To try to keep everyone as healthy as possible during cold and flu season, I try to make sure everyone washes their hands as much as possible and I try to feed us healthy foods with lots of fruits and vegetables. We also try to stay away from the member of the family who's sick, although that's harder for me since I'm the one who's the primary caregiver. I just try to wash my hands a lot and not touch my eyes, nose or mouth with unwashed hands and try to get as much sleep as possible to keep my defenses up because if I get sick, we'll this leads us to the next chapter….

When You Get Sick

When you're feeling sick, life gets very difficult. It's so hard to try to take care of your children when you're feeling sick and exhausted. It depends on how sick I'm feeling, but if I'm really doing bad, I have to enlist the help of my husband. No other family member wants to come over to help because of course nobody wants to be exposed. I get a flu shot every year to try to minimize any illnesses I might get and I wash my hands religiously, to the point where they get very dry in the winter. But there have still been times where I just need to get up to bed and David needs to take over for me.

In fact, I remember one day when Alex was a baby. David and Zach had left to visit one of our friends and I stayed home with Alex. I wasn't feeling good, which was the reason I decided to stay home in the first place. For some reason, I got the worst headache of my whole life. I had to lie down – I couldn't even stay upright. I put Alex in a play seat that had lots of toys built all around it and I just lied down on the carpet in front of him. Thankfully, David called to check up on me and could tell by the way I sounded that I wasn't doing well. He came home and took care of both the children while I went to bed – bless him!

Gadgets

Thankfully my children know how to use all sorts of gadgets, because I definitely don't! Over the years from Gameboy, DS, PSP and Wii to iPods, iPads and iPhones, I have always told them that they have to figure it out because I haven't a clue. And, unbelievably, they always do. It's amazing how easily kids of this generation learn to operate these gadgets. It's great they understand technology so well and so easily because they need to in our information-oriented world. Now the problem becomes how much time they spend on these devices. Look around and you see how many people seem to be constantly on their smartphones. It seems that nobody can just stand in line and wait anymore without having to scroll through something. I've even noticed when friends are together, instead of talking face-to-face, they are texting each other – and they are less than a foot apart!

So, there's definitely a balance that needs to be met. Children have to learn how to operate all the newest gadgets because it's become so much a part of daily life, which will most likely continue into the future. They also need to keep up-to-date with the newest devices that periodically enter the market. This is imperative if they are to operate effectively in the business world. However, we need to teach them social skills, which are just as important in business, as in life. They need to know how to communicate verbally and to read nonverbal cues, such as body language, facial expressions and tone of voice. If we can teach them this balance, all these gadgets now and in the future can assist them in their daily life instead of being controlled by them.

Rushing to the Emergency Room, Again

There used to be a time in my sons' lives when we made so many trips to the Emergency Room that when we walked in, the attendant behind the desk would say "hi, Mrs. George, how are you doing today?" Well, not quite, but it sure did feel that way.

Now, is this mostly an issue with having sons or does this happen with young children in general? As the boys have gotten older, there aren't as many trips to the ER, at least not for them (David has been there with broken ribs and a broken foot and I have for a broken foot also, and after fainting in a restaurant up in the mountains). But when the boys were younger, they got hurt a lot. It seems that they would just play too hard and didn't know their strength and someone would end up getting hurt or they would get really sick and it would be outside of doctor's office hours (of course).

There was a time when our family went to the ER so much in such a short period of time that social services called our house. During that time, Zach ended up in the ER with a cut on his forehead that required stitches because he had been dancing at his grandparent's house and had fallen and hit the edge of a wood table. Then I broke my foot while David was out of town while I was taking out the trash one night (who would have thought taking out the trash could be so dangerous!). Then, my mom came over to help me take care of the boys while my foot was broken, and she accidentally kneeled on Alex's ankle while she was changing his diaper on the ground. He started wailing and we had to take him to the ER to see if his ankle was broken. You should have seen us walking in there!! I had crutches and a boot, Zach had a bandage on his forehead and baby Alex was wailing! We looked like a comedy of errors! And all this happened within a two-week period. The only person in our family that was uninjured was David, so social services called to make sure everything was fine in our household!

Then there was the time we took Zach to the ER when he was a little over a year old. He had a high fever and was miserable. We called our doctor's answering service and the doctor told us to take him to the ER. Now you know you can sometimes wait awhile in the ER. Well here's a tip for you: if your child throws up in the waiting room, they'll take you to the back quickly. Then as we were waiting to get into an actual room, David was holding him and he threw up all over him again! Poor David!! He kept having to wipe off his clothes with wet cloths. Poor Zach – he was so miserable! After the second time Zach got sick, they got a doctor to see him in a hurry.

We have all broken some bones and ended up in the ER. I already mentioned David's ribs, foot and my foot. Zach broke his collarbone when he was five and that was very scary. David and the boys were horsing around in our living room and Alex accidentally fell on Zach. He happened to do it at an angle which snapped Zach's collarbone. Zach was on the ground wailing and he couldn't move. We were smart enough to know not to force the issue when he was really acting like he couldn't move. We couldn't get him into the car because he couldn't sit up, so we had no other choice than to call an ambulance. That was so scary having an ambulance take him away.

Then Alex broke his right arm when he was eight. He was playing at a friend's house and was moving backwards without looking back. Unfortunately, there was a bike behind him. One of the kids tried to warn him but it was too late. He started falling and put his arm out to catch his fall. Unfortunately, it was his right arm. He had to have kids at school write for him when they were doing classwork and I had to write down his homework at home. He did have fun getting everyone to sign his cast, though.

Then Zach broke one of his fingers when he was eleven. Basketball season was just beginning, and he broke it at practice. He and his coach didn't realize it was broken, so he kept on practicing! I wasn't at the practice, so I didn't know anything was wrong until I picked him up. Unfortunately, he had to sit out most of that season because it takes so long for a break to heal. He showed up at almost every game, though, to cheer his team on. Then he was able to play about two games before the season was over.

So now, as I've mentioned before, we're making less trips to the ER and we like it that way. Also, the last couple of trips have not been for the boys, but for David and me. So, it looks like David and I need to watch ourselves – we're getting older (bummer) and a bit more fragile (extra bummer).

Saying "I Love You" and Other Kissy Stuff

When our boys were younger, it was easier to tell them I loved them and to kiss them and show them lots of affection – they liked it. But of course, as they got older they lost patience with this sort of thing. It starts with them wanting to be less affectionate in public and eventually becomes not wanting to be as affectionate even at home. Not only did they become less affectionate, but they didn't want me to be as demonstrative physically or verbally. Because of this, I started to love the mornings. When I went to their rooms to wake them up, I could give them a few kisses – they were too tired to fight it. And really – I think they secretly liked it!

Now, I know I don't tell them I love them as much as I still probably should. My sons don't even want to walk with me anymore, or more accurately, for anyone to see them walking with me. Because of this, I only walk them to a locked gate going from our neighborhood to the school because I have the only key. I then tell them to have a good day and watch as they enter the school field. Whenever I do say I love them, they either roll their eyes, say "yeah" or "I know". It's a very rare thing for me to ever hear "me too" back. But it's OK – they're growing older, becoming more independent and need to pull away from mom to feel like young men. I'll just keep bombarding them in the mornings, when they don't have the strength to fight it.

Chaos

Living with children inevitably means living with chaos. Before children, there actually used to be times when my life was fairly orderly. After children ... not so much. Here are some examples of some of the chaos that has been part of our day-to-day lives.

- Breaking my foot the night after my husband left for a week-long business trip to New York City, while trying to take care of a newborn and his 22-month old brother. Needless to say, I needed to rally the support of numerous family members and friends because I couldn't pick up Alex while hobbling around on crutches and he was still feeding in the middle of the night.

- Trying to pack all the requirements you need for a baby and a toddler when visiting two different sets of families on Christmas Eve, let alone the presents and food/drink items you are bringing. Let alone trying to remember everything and just trying to get it all into the car. Then unpacking most of it at the 1st place and then packing most of that back up when it's time to leave for the 2nd place, along with the new toys for the boys. Then repeating this process at the 2nd place and then again when you get home exhausted ... and, no, the boys did not fall asleep in the car on the way home so now you have to put them to bed and they're cranky.

- Walking home with Zach one day from kindergarten, we stopped on the grass under a tree for some reason. I forget now because what happened next erased all memory of what we were doing before. I was wearing sandals and I felt some itchy, tingling sensation. When I looked down, I noticed a bunch of ants walking on my foot. Then I realized why – I was standing on a dead rat!!! I screamed and ran and took off my sandals when we got to our front door. Then I hopped upstairs and washed my foot for about an hour in our bathtub. Then I had to bleach our bathtub and spray it with disinfectant. I was, of course, going to throw away those sandals until my neighbor told me she would take them (huh?!) If anybody ever asks me what the grossest, most disgusting thing was that's happened in my life, this would be it.

- And speaking of rats, one morning our puppy was outside and having an absolutely delightful time in our back yard. He was ready to come back in, when I noticed something hanging from his mouth … a dead rat! Yes, a dead rat!! Our cute little puppy was having a ton of fun playing with a dead rat. Of course, this is all happening as I'm trying to make breakfast and get the boys out the door for school. To make a long story short, that cute little puppy got a trip to our vet for a bath before I could even get near him again. Do you get the feeling I don't like rats? Especially dead ones!

- Near the end of a fun and very busy year, when I ended up being the head room mom in both my sons' classes (without realizing that was going to happen), I was planning and preparing two different parties for their teachers, three different class lunches, two end-of-school parties for the children and two end-of-year scrapbook gifts for the teachers. By the end of that school year, I really needed a vacation! Although, I do have to admit, it was a very fun year!

- Just some nice, random Sunday morning, as I'm making pancakes (a Sunday morning ritual – from scratch, mind you – not that I'm bragging), one of my sons just happens to spill his hot chocolate on our living room carpet. Hot chocolate on a cream-colored carpet! Well, if that doesn't wake you up quickly, nothing will!

- On one of our skiing trips to Big Bear, Alex, then about 8 years old, decided he wanted to try some cheesecake with strawberries after eating pizza for dinner. We told him to watch out because that was a lot of food. Well, I paid for that mistake dearly. When we got back to our hotel room, Alex had to go to the bathroom. After he did his business, he got sick. We've taught both the boys how to lift the toilet seat and try to aim when they get sick. Alex somehow forgot this lesson and to this day, I am not sure how he did this. There was pink vomit sprayed all over the bathroom – the back of the door, each of the four walls, the bathtub, the bathtub curtain, the floor and a bit on the toilet. Guess who got to clean it up? And guess what else? NO MORE CHEESECAKE AFTER PIZZA – EVER !!!!

So these are just some examples and I could go on and on and on, but this chapter is already getting too long and I wouldn't want to bore you. You learn to live with a certain amount of chaos when you have two sons, a cat, a dog and a husband who sometimes acts like a third child.

What About You?

The Woman in You

Many times, you have to remind yourself that you are a woman, not just a mother. You must remind yourself that you're also your husband's wife. David and I would have date nights periodically. We were lucky that we had family nearby who were willing to watch Zach and Alex while we went out. Sometimes we would just go for a casual dinner and other times, usually for special events like birthdays or anniversaries, we would go to an elegant restaurant. For special birthdays, we would even spend the night at a nice local hotel that's attached to one of our favorite restaurants. These evenings would allow us to reconnect outside of our everyday world and remind us what it was like before kids – what initially attracted us to each other. We would try to talk about topics other than the children. Although it's hard not to mention the children especially during an overnight stay, so that was OK, we would just try to have that not be the main topic.

Many books and magazines talk about making sure you have regular "date nights". That is great, and I think it was even more important when the boys were younger and things seemed more hectic. But now we don't have actual "date nights" quite as regularly. However, we don't stress about it because we find we connect during everyday moments of respite. Sometimes we have unexpected moments when the kids are finished eating dinner, but David and I continue our mealtime and just talk about our day and funny or topical things that may be going on at the time. Even having a few minutes at the end of the day to touch base or call or e-mail each other reminds us that we are on the same team – we are working for the same end result. I think those things happening routinely can keep a strong bond along with trying to keep up with "date nights".

Recently David and I got the chance to go away for a weekend. We were meeting up with some friends from David's college and it was a grown-up event – a lobster and wine feast at a winery in Napa Valley. The grandparents agreed to have Zach and Alex stay with them and David and I jumped at the opportunity. We had a wonderful time!! We were able to relax and remember ourselves before children. Also, getting together with a bunch of old friends reminded us of our younger selves – you feel a certain sense of vitality after that. The whole weekend I felt I was being taken care of, which is a wonderful thing when you are usually the one taking care of others. We returned refreshed and very happy to see the boys. The boys meantime had a great time with the grandparents – swimming, making clay objects, playing games, watching movies, etc. The grandparents loved spending that much uninterrupted time with the boys, especially now that they don't usually see them as often as they used to. It was a win-win situation all around.

Also, you can capture moments when you're with your kids, but they're preoccupied, to connect. For example, during one recent Father's Day we went to a beautiful beach and after playing catch with them, having a picnic and watching a breathtaking sunset, we went down to the water so the boys could play for awhile. David and I watched them while sitting on some rocks and visiting. We talked about things we hadn't talked about in awhile – it was date-conversation. It was really nice because we were there with the boys, watching the boys, but we were connecting again as individuals and learning a bit more about each other.

You also need to connect with your girlfriends every once in awhile. Some of the mom friends I made would make plans with me to go get coffee and visit after we dropped off the kids at school. I would normally walk after dropping off the kids and eventually I would make plans with my mom friends to go walking instead of getting coffee. This way we would be exercising and taking care of ourselves while we got to visit. It was great to get a chance to vent and compare notes regarding motherhood without constant interruptions. We would also talk about other topics, too, bonding us as friends, not just fellow mothers.

When people ask me what's new in my life, I realize my answer has a lot to do with what's currently going on with the boys. That's because that really is my day-to-day life. I do keep up with current events and am interested in politics, but my personal life is very involved with the boys' school life and extra-curricular activities and that's fine, as long as I do find those moments to connect with and remember my former and constantly evolving self.

Taking Care of Yourself

Before children, and even when they were younger, I took better care of myself. I used to give myself a facial once a week, do some exercises in the evenings, give myself pedicures and manicures, etc. Now that they're older, the evenings are busier and they're awake longer. They now have sports activities that will sometimes push dinner back until after 7. Then there's homework to finish, showers, reading, washing dishes, cleaning up, etc. They'll be in bed by around 8:30, but they won't actually fall asleep sometimes until 10:30. By the time everything is finished, I'm just too pooped to give myself a facial or do exercises, let alone worrying about my feet or hands. So now I use a scrub lotion about once a week instead of the usual facial to try to simulate a mini-facial. I'll sometimes do abbreviated exercises or stretches, although I do walk in the mornings. As for my feet and hands, I just keep my nails clipped and if there's a special event, I might put some polish on, but I really don't have time for consistent upkeep.

When it comes to clothes, I usually just buy what I really need. Once shirts or pants have faded or begin to look too worn out, I go out and buy enough to replace them. Somehow it always seems like by the end of the day, I have some type of spot on my shirts. Throughout the course of the day, with cooking, cleaning, juggling myriad things around, I've gotten some type of spot on me. Then there's the darn cat. She's always getting holes in our shirts. One of my favorite shirts got a hole right in the front because I was holding her and she put her claw right into my shirt. I've given up picking her up.

I look admirably at those women who always seem to look put-together. I don't know how they do it. It just takes so much work. Believe me, it's not that I don't like to pamper myself or be pampered, but there's just so much else to do and so many other things that really seem to take precedence on the priority list.

From Boardroom to Playroom

Ok, well not board room, more like conference room – whatever. Anyway, before many of us became moms, we had started a career. I used to work in advertising and was climbing the corporate ladder in the account and media departments before I became pregnant. Many of us continue to work after having children, whether by necessity or choice.

After Zach was born, I went back to work when he was about eight months old. We had moved to Irvine from Sacramento before he was born and I didn't have a job, I had just done temp work in Orange County before he was born. So, I had to go out looking for a job. We had a great situation in that my parents were willing to take care of Zach two days a week, so I only needed childcare for three days a week. In addition to the cost savings, I liked the fact that Zach was getting bonding time with my parents. I was glad to go back to work because unfortunately, Zach had colic. If you've ever experienced a baby with colic, you know how unbearable it can be. Zach's wasn't only in the evening, it was any time he was awake and not feeding. We tried all kinds of different remedies, but nothing worked. Colic usually lasts for about four months. Zach had colic for six. So, it felt like a break for me to be at work. I could concentrate and go to the bathroom whenever I felt like it and have uninterrupted time while eating lunch, and they were paying me.

I stayed at that job until Alex was born. After that, I knew it was going to be too hard to work full-time with a newborn and a toddler who was 1 ½. I tried to convince them to bring me back to work part-time, but they wouldn't agree. So, David and I made the decision that I would stay home. Although it was definitely challenging, I was glad I had the opportunity to be a stay-at-home mom. Once they got older, I started looking for work again, especially when David's agency closed, but I never got hired. The high unemployment rate didn't help and by then I had been out of the workforce for a decade and that didn't make me particularly marketable. So now I'm trying to make my millions with this book (ha, ha – can you tell all your friends they should buy it?)

I Never Wear Heels Anymore (And I'm 5'1")

I've noticed that now that I don't go to a job, I don't wear heels very often. I used to wear heels all the time, partly because I'm short. But now I'm always wearing flats of some sort. Most of this has to do with the fact that I mostly wear casual clothes now. Also, as the boys have grown, I've been on my feet and running around most of the time. Heels just aren't comfortable unless you're sitting most of the day.

It's gotten to the point that when I do dress up and wear heels, it feels strange to me. Those who know me well know I have a tendency toward clumsiness, so now when I wear heels I have to be careful and walk slowly and really watch where I'm going lest I trip.

I went to a birthday lunch recently for one of my dear friends and wore sandals with heels. I almost tripped while walking down the stairs. I guess I better go out more often with nice clothes and heels just to keep me in practice.

Things I Don't Spend Money on Anymore

Manicures

I never really did that much before because I really don't think they feel good and I preferred to just do it myself anyway, but now I don't even give them to myself because why bother – my nails are just going to break and chip anyway because of all the dish washing.

Coloring my hair

I do not have the time or money to sit in a salon while a hairstylist colors my hair. There was a time that I did and I would even get highlights (fancy!). But now I get color from a box and do it myself at home. And you know what? I get compliments on the color of my hair, even from my hairstylist. She evens mentions how healthy my hair is. So, I get to save money and time and it's really not even noticeable.

Cappuccinos

I do very rarely because it's just easier and less expensive to make coffee at home. One of David's and the boys' favorite gifts to give me is a Starbucks card so I will splurge. It's funny how long one of these cards will last me, though, even when it's just $10 – I can keep it for six months!

Dry Cleaning

Most of what I wear now is wash-&-wear. I'm only wearing something that needs to be dry-cleaned if it's a special occasion. Therefore, I'm usually just going to the dry-cleaners for David's clothes and since he's in advertising, he gets to wear jeans and T-shirts (nice, stylish ones) to work most of the time. So, the local dry-cleaner doesn't see me that often and our bank account is thankful for that.

Fancy Clothes, Shoes, etc.
See "dry-cleaning" above

Pantyhose
Well kind of self-explanatory when I don't wear fancy clothes much, but it also seems that my fancy clothes are all pants. I'm not quite sure why and I've never really thought about it before now, but that's just the way it's turned out. Maybe I'll have to look at buying a skirt, soon. But I'm just not used to pantyhose anymore.

Things I Do Spend Money on Now

Boys' Sneakers
Their feet just keep growing and growing …

Boys' Jeans
How do they get holes in the knees so quickly?

Allowance
We do tie them to chores because we feel it teaches them to work to make money and that if you want more money, you have to do more chores or come up with a plan to make money (which Alex has, by the way – he used to set up a table in our neighborhood and sell toys he didn't want anymore – very clever!)

Pet Food and Supplies
The boys did talk us into getting a cat. And then, a dog.

Activities for the Boys
These have varied over the years from all kinds of sports (soccer, baseball, basketball, football, swimming, tennis, Tae Kwon Do, etc.) to interests such as guitar lessons, Spanish classes, lego building classes, robot building classes, video making classes and various camps. I feel this is money well-spent because it has exposed them to many different things and has helped them to define and narrow their interests.

Vacations

We don't go hog-wild, but I feel this is money well-spent because this gives us time as a family to get away from the hustle and bustle of everyday life and share time and have adventures together. These moments will continue to be special memories and help us all to strengthen our bond.

Gadgets

Through the years it's been Gameboys, Gamecube, DS's, PSP's, Nintendo Wii, iPods, laptops, iPads, iPhones, etc. I know this will just continue. As the boys have gotten older, they want these gadgets instead of traditional toys for their birthdays and Christmas. Now they've started to ask for money because the gadgets are getting more and more expensive and are too much for us to buy them for birthdays or Christmas. So this way, they save up their own money so they can buy it for themselves. This also teaches them how to save and delay gratification.

Beware the Hazards of Being a Mom

When you become a mom, you're going to find that you get hurt more than you used to, especially when you have two rambunctious, energetic boys. When your children are toddlers, you might get hit with toys that are flying through the air as your kids research the principles of aerodynamics. You will inevitably trip on toys, especially when walking across the floor holding the laundry basket. Don't even get me started on how good it feels to step on a Lego piece with all your weight (yikes!) Then there are just the accidents that seem to happen from having youngsters around – they don't always just hurt themselves or each other – you can get caught in the crossfire.

Just the other day I was getting ready to take the boys to the park. We were meeting some friends there and I was getting snacks and water together. We were about to leave and I asked the boys to come get their waters. I was holding a water bottle as Zach decided to run towards me and jump up to grab the bottle. I had no idea he was going to do this, mind you. In the process, he somehow slammed the bottle into my cheek in his exuberance. I was not happy! I had a bruise that had a scrape over it that was bleeding a bit – great – right on my face. It took a couple of weeks to completely go away.

And it's not just hazardous being a mom, dads are in danger, too. Once David was opening the car door for Zach and Zach jumped up, and in the process, head-slammed David in the jaw! It slightly dislocated David's jaw. He had to go to the doctor and it took months for it to get back to normal. We've told Zach he's forbidden to jump around us (kidding – but … you kind of want to). They wonder why I back away when they get too close to me ….

Feeling It More Than They Do

When you're a mom, you feel your child's pain. You usually feel it stronger than they do. When they're crying because they fell or they're getting a shot, etc. you can almost feel the physical pain and you feel bad for them, too. They usually get over it well before you do. How many of us have told our children when punishing them that it hurts us as much as it does them? The children probably don't believe us, but it's true. As they get older, the hurts get bigger and deeper, becoming more emotional hurts and disappointments than just cuts and bruises. It also gets harder to help alleviate the pain and you realize that you do need to step back many times and let them work it out, or work through it, for them to grow, mature and become self-sufficient in the world.

I recently had an incident with my one of my sons that I think may be hurting me more than him. His best friend of two years decided out of the blue that he didn't want to hang out with my son anymore, but hang with another kid. He abruptly shut my son out of his life and ignored him. My son was rightfully surprised, hurt and confused by his actions. I was too, especially because his mom was a very good mom-friend of mine (one of my best) and our husbands got along really well also. We would go to each other's houses and visit and have wine and cheese, the mom and I would go out for girls' night together and my husband even went on a boat trip with the other dad. So what was going on? Why did this happen so suddenly, without warning? I was wondering if this boy was telling his parents what was going on. What was the version he was telling them? What were they saying to him?

Another incident that happened with my other son when he was in first grade left a painful memory for me for a long time, while it seemed not to affect my son too much, thankfully. He was the only boy in his first-grade class to not be invited to another classmate's birthday party. All the boys were talking about going to the party and started to tease him about not being invited. Thankfully, the teacher found out what was going on and talked to the boys. I was so hurt and angry! Not only did this mother purposefully exclude my son from the birthday party, but a couple of months before, she had called me a day before my son's party to see if her son could still come to my son's party. You see, I had invited him, and she decided not to RSVP. Then her son begged her to go. I was very welcoming and said by all means he could come. Now she had the nerve to exclude my son?! And he was the only boy, as I mentioned, that was not invited in the class. Furthermore, our sons were both in Cub Scouts together! I had such a bad time with this incident, but I didn't want my son to see how much it affected me and I wanted to minimize its affect on him as much as possible. So, my husband and I kept him busy all weekend doing fun things like going to dinner, going to the movies, playing board games and going to the park. This way we were also able to spend a lot of time with him and his brother and shower him with attention and affection.

The Kid in You

You might find yourself feeling like a kid again, sometimes when you're watching your children or experiencing certain events with them. There were numerous times when they brought out the kid in me, and I hadn't felt that way in a long time. Some of the things that brought me back to my old kid-self were:

Bedtime stories and songs

I really loved reading fairy tales and singing bedtime songs to them, like "Twinkle, Twinkle Little Star". We had this great book that had lots of fairy tales. It had the ones I knew growing up but a bunch of new ones as well.

Swinging on swings

I would have fun getting on the swing next to them and pretending to try to swing higher than them. I remember how exhilarating and free it felt to swing when I was a kid. One difference between swinging now and when I was a child, though, is that now it makes me a bit dizzy and nauseous – strange.

Learning about my sons' interests

I never knew so much about trucks and dinosaurs before and I never had an interest in them. However, reading about them to my sons taught me much about them and I was surprised at how interested I became. Now I've lost most of that knowledge, but it was there when I was reading it to them. I'm sure there will be new subjects they will introduce me to in the future.

Watching (and liking) some of their movies and TV shows

When we first started popcorn night on Friday nights, my sons were around 5 and 3. So we watched movies appropriate for young children, like lots of Disney movies. My favorite movie from that time period was *Aristocats*. It is a cute movie about stray cats living in Paris and a nice, wealthy widow who rescues a bunch of them. Some other movies I like from that time were the *Land Before Time* series, which were about some cute children dinosaurs and all their adventures. Some of the TV shows they used to watch that I liked were *Sesame Street, Dragon Tales* and *Spongebob Squarepants*. Now they've gotten me into the *Harry Potter* books and movies and I sometimes watch some of their TV shows, although they're not quite as cute as the ones they watched when they were younger.

Going on Strike

Well, I've never actually done this, just dreamed about it – about telling the hubby and the boys "that's it and I'm not going to take it anymore!" I'm sick of constantly preparing food, cleaning up afterward, asking the boys to pick up after themselves, dealing with all the clutter, dealing with the boys' fighting and snarky comments and just generally feeling like a maid, cook and referee in my own house.

I dream about dramatically storming off and then spending a night or two at a fancy hotel by myself. I would order room service and read a book or flip through some magazines and go to bed when I want to without having to yell at anyone about going to bed themselves. Then I would wake up in the morning when I wanted to, go out to the balcony and have a quiet morning, not having to rush to wake anyone up, prepare breakfast and make sure they're ready for the day and out the door on time.

But, (sigh), I just could never do it. I've half-way threatened maybe a couple of times, but the farthest I've gone is to hole myself in my room for a little while. I'll go up there, lock the door if I'm really fed up and turn on the TV to watch what I want to see or flip through some magazines for a little while. After I've decompressed a bit and everyone knows I mean business, I come downstairs and re-enter the fray.

I Don't Have Privacy Anymore

I decided to write this chapter after I went upstairs to use our bathroom and not 5 seconds later, David came barging through the door. Mind you, we had been downstairs for the last couple of hours and David didn't need me for anything during most of that time. But somehow, once I go to use our bathroom he suddenly, urgently needs to tell me something of utmost importance! I have noticed this pattern with my children, too. Is this mostly an issue of living with men? All of a sudden, they notice that the wife/mother is no longer in sight and they panic because they feel they urgently need something from her.

I have noticed this type of behavior whenever I am in the bathroom, changing clothes, taking a shower, brushing my teeth or using the telephone. These are times I would really like just a few minutes of privacy – just a few minutes of not having someone watching me, asking me questions or requesting something from me. Just now, as I'm writing this, I got interrupted by one of my sons yelling a question to me. I stopped to help him because I thought he was doing homework. Turns out he just had a question. So, I guess I need to add "trying to write" on my list of activities I'd like some privacy for – sheesh!

Stop Judging Me

When you are a mother, there will be times when you inevitably feel judged. I try not to do this with other moms because I know the other side of the fence. There were numerous times when one of my boys would be misbehaving or throwing a tantrum in public. When your children go ballistic, people tend to look at you and wonder what you did to cause it. Almost every single time it is nothing you did except that your child is not getting their way.

There were some times when one of my boys would be misbehaving and I could sense that an adult didn't approve of the way I was handling it or disciplining him. What they might not have known, however, is that I was choosing to fight certain battles, not every single one, or that there might have been an extenuating circumstance regarding my reaction.

Bottom line is, it's not their business unless I'm abusing or harming my child. They don't know the history and the circumstances around an event, so they don't really have enough information to make a fair judgment, although many people do this. I try very hard not to be one of those people. When I see and hear a child having a tantrum, for example, I don't stare at the child and his or her parent. I just silently thank the heavens that it's not happening to me (this time).

When Mom's Happy, Everyone's Happy

We all know that when we're feeling cranky and run-down, we tend to snap at our loved ones more often and that makes them feel bad and us feel worse. So, we need to make sure to do things that will make us happy whenever we can. Not only do our children need time-outs sometimes, but we do as well. There have been times when I've holed myself in my room for a little while to get much needed peace and quiet. There have been times when I've just laid down on the sofa for about 15 minutes because I really need to just de-stress for a bit.

What are your favorite ways to recharge? You might even want to make a list of them, so you can look it over when you're really feeling frantic or burned out and need some ideas to bring yourself up. Here's a partial list:

- Candlelit bath with a good book and/or a glass of wine
- Reading a good or fun book in bed or a nice, quiet, cozy spot
- Going for a walk
- Sitting out on the patio or porch
- Calling a friend and venting and laughing
- Perusing your favorite social media sites
- Taking a cat-nap
- Meditating
- Listening to your favorite music
- Giving yourself a pedicure, manicure and/or facial

- Watching a funny TV show or movie
- Eating some really good-quality chocolate
- Sipping some calming herbal tea

I personally love cat-naps or just laying down on the sofa for 15 minutes or so. Sometimes in the evening I like to give myself a pedicure and sip a glass of wine. I love watching funny TV shows and movies, although I rarely have time to watch a whole movie. I also love to read magazines for about 10 minutes – it's a fun way to relax without taking too much time, energy or concentration. These are just simple ways for me to feel better without a lot of time, money or effort.

Teaching Them

Explaining Illnesses/Financial Hardships and Such

Life isn't always so peachy-keen as we would like it to be or our children believe it is. There are some difficult situations that come along that we have to explain to our children without glazing over it too rose-colored or making them feel too frightened from it. We always tried to give Zach and Alex age-appropriate explanations and answer their questions.

For example, when Zach's and Alex's grandfather was diagnosed with colon cancer, he started to not feel well after chemo treatments and started looking differently – he lost weight and with one set of chemo cocktails, developed a bad rash on his face. He couldn't be around anyone who was the least bit sick. So we explained to the boys that grandpa was sick but he was taking medicine to get better. Because he was sick, he couldn't be around anyone else that was sick or it could make him sicker. We explained that the medicine made him look the way he did. We didn't mention the word "cancer" because they were still fairly young and we thought the word would unduly scare them. Now, we have mentioned cancer and they don't really ask many questions. They'll understand it more when they get older.

Sometimes your children develop chronic conditions which you all have to deal with. Our experience continues to be that you give them enough information to answer their questions without alarming them. They will continue to be given more information as they get older and as their questions increase. An optimistic attitude on your part helps them and you put it into perspective. A lot of people deal with a lot of things that we have no clue about.

There are also sometimes events that happen that can cause financial hardships. This happened for us when David's office was closed during the recession/financial meltdown period of late 2008. All we told the children at that time was that dad decided he wanted another job and was looking for one. We told them that most people had to be more careful with their money now because they didn't have as much as they used to, including us. So, we all had to watch how much we spent. They seemed to do a good job of understanding what we were saying, although they continued to be more avid consumers than we would have liked. But it was a good lesson for them to learn.

The main thing to remember when going through trying times and explaining it to your kids is that we can all come through tough times stronger. Like we've all heard, what doesn't kill us makes us stronger. That's a good lesson for kids to learn so they can develop more confidence and ultimately become resilient. As they successfully meet new challenges and handle more problems, remind them of what a good job they did so they can remember their past successes when met with new tough situations. This teaches them that they are able to cope with challenging circumstances, which is always a good thing to remember in the future.

Values

You have to decide as a family what values are important to you that you want to impart to your children. Your routines can help enforce the values that are especially important to your family. For example, family is very important to us, so we make sure we spend a good deal of time together each week, try to eat dinner together most nights and make sure Zach and Alex see their grandparents, aunts, uncles and cousins on a regular basis. Education is another important value to us, so we make sure they realize the importance of giving their best effort to their schoolwork and striving for the best grades they are capable of.

We would discuss with our children what our values are and why they are so important to us. For example, we've taught our children to be honest because if they lie, we will probably eventually find out and then that erodes our trust – we won't be able to know if they are lying or telling the truth, so we won't be able to trust what they tell us anymore. Another side to honesty is not cheating. We've taught them that if you cheat, you haven't fairly earned that grade, so you can't feel proud of yourself for it – it's a hollow success. Also, you won't get the help you might need because it looks like you understand everything.

We've also tried to teach them not to take things for granted and to be thankful for what they have. We want them to understand that there are a lot of people in the world who don't have as much as we do and that we need to give back to the world. For this, we gather together items that we don't use any longer, like toys or books, or clothes that don't fit anymore but are still in good condition. Then we give these items to charity. Also, we send money to aid organizations when disasters occur, like Hurricane Katrina, the tsunami in Asia, the earthquake in Haiti, etc. The boys gather their own money to include in this.

We've also tried to teach them to think for themselves and to discover for themselves which values are important to them. We realize that as they mature, they may not continue to always have the same values as we do. Although that will feel disappointing, we do want them to be true to themselves and find their own place in the world. To that end, we try to teach them to be independent thinkers and respect others' opinions.

Internet Safety

Our school and local police department host an Internet Safety meeting each year to explain the potential dangers of internet use for our children and what we can do about it as parents. The goal is not to completely keep our children off the internet but to give them information and a sense of empowerment, so they can use it safely and effectively. If you forbid them to use the internet entirely, they may use it at a friend's house or somewhere else where you cannot supervise them. Therefore, we need to teach them how to use it properly and safely.

The following are some of the risks for children and teens accessing the internet: they can be exposed to inappropriate material, they can go into a questionable chat room like those regarding "dating, companionship, relationships and sexual activity," they can be communicating with someone who is misrepresenting himself/herself, they could decide to meet someone face-to-face who they don't know, and they could be bullied or harassed online.

To reduce these risks, you'll need to teach them general rules of safety and stress that computer, laptop and smartphone use are privileges that can be taken away if they're not used responsibly. Next, you'll need to set up parental controls through your service provider to restrict which sites can be accessed. Our police department advises to "set up a computer administrator account and control the users" so only you can delete internet history and control content settings.

Finally, teach your children the following rules and guidelines:

- Anything they post online (words or pictures) is out in cyberspace forever. Even if your child deletes them, they could have previously been captured and saved by anyone. Then they could reappear later, negatively affecting them.
- Schools, colleges and potential employers sometimes check the internet for background searches. This is a very important message to communicate to them. There have been instances where someone has posted pictures or written about a questionable activity, like partying, thinking it would be fun for their friends to see. Then when a college admissions officer or a hiring manager at a company do a search of them, they see what all the friends saw and decide to take a pass on that person.
- Never give out your first or last name, address, phone numbers, age, date of birth, gender, school name or location (even the city it's in), parents' names or phone numbers or mention if you are home alone. It is also recommended that they don't give out personal descriptions, habits, hobbies or hangouts. Pedophiles can use this information to try to gain their trust and make them think they understand them.
- Never post a picture of themselves. They can use an avatar instead.
- Don't let your child be part of video conference calls where they can be seen by unknown people.
- Of course, never, ever arrange a face-to-face meeting with someone they have met on the Internet.
- Realize that people aren't always who they say they are online. That fun, cool 16-year-old boy your daughter is talking to could actually be a creepy 56-year-old man (no offense to 56-year-old men).
- They need your approval to take any surveys and be very cautious of these because they can give too much personal information.

- If they are being bullied or harassed by someone online, they need to tell you, a teacher, a police office or some other responsible adult. These messages can slip into a crime category and need to be dealt with. Of course, do not bully or harass anyone else.

- If your child sets up an account through a social networking site, it should be on the condition that you also set up an account and you are added as a friend or follower, so you can view your child's page anytime. Your child needs to select the strictest privacy settings so only friends can view it, not just anyone. Also, your child should never accept someone who is trying to become a friend on their site that they do not personally know. You not only have to be wary of pedophiles, but of identity theft.

- Never exchange passwords. There have been a number of instances where friends share passwords then they get into a fight and a former friend uses the shared password to log onto the other person's page. Then they can say a lot of inappropriate things or worse and mayhem follows.

- Sexting is NEVER allowed. Beyond the fact that these pictures can be sent to anyone after they are out there, there can be very serious consequences including charges of disseminating child pornography! This is strictly off-limits!

Good and Bad Habits

They say your children are always watching you and that you are always role-modeling appropriate (or not) behavior to them (uh oh!) So, it makes sense that you want to highlight your good habits and hide or at least downplay your bad ones. I don't think it's necessary to completely hide your bad habits because there's an element of dishonesty in that and our children need to know that we're human, too. I think it makes them feel secure knowing that we are also fallible and that everyone makes mistakes sometimes.

One of the good habits I have that I show my children daily is reading. I love to read and I read every day because it's relaxing to me. So, they always see me reading magazines, newspapers, a book or something. David also reads every day and enjoys it. Imagine our chagrin when both our sons complain about reading. They are required to read for a certain amount of time or a certain number of pages every day. But they just don't relish it the way David and I do and we don't quite understand. As they find more books they're interested in, it's getting a bit better. But I do hope we get to a time when they enjoy reading just for the sheer pleasure of it.

Another good habit I have is flossing every day (I know, I know, but I actually do – I'm not just lying to my dentist). This is a habit I got into and I cannot go to bed now without flossing. I got David into the habit, too, but the boys resist. Their dentist and I try to show them how to floss and tell them how important it is. I try to floss their teeth, but they complain and wiggle and move their heads around and it's an unpleasant job. I try to warn them that they'll get cavities if they don't take care of their teeth, including flossing, but they act like I'm torturing them. Again, I hope that someday this habit will somehow get under their skin, so to speak.

Now, not all my habits are good ones, I'm sorry to say. They also see me being lazy sometimes, eating chips in front of the TV, sleeping in too late on weekends, telling a white lie every so often, etc. You don't need to know all of them. As I said before, this just shows we're all human and that nobody's perfect, so I hope instead of picking up my bad habits (although I do see them exhibit a few of these), that it will just teach them that they can't be absolutely perfect. They can strive to get as close as is humanly possible. Just not to let it eat at them too much in the areas where they fail.

Manners

Of course, it's important to teach our children good manners so they're seen in a good light by others and function well in a civilized society. To that end, we taught them early to say "please" and "thank you". We used to get many compliments on their using these words in the appropriate situations. As they've gotten older, they've gotten a bit lax about this and don't care as much, so we have to get on them a bit. We also taught them to send thank you cards when someone gives them a gift. The way we do it in our family is that if the family member is present when you open their gift and you express your gratitude in person, then you don't need to send a note. But I make sure they send thanks to friends, even if they were present, and any family members who didn't receive a personal thanks.

Table manners are very important and we've always worked on this. The boys generally hold their utensils properly, don't put their elbows on the table and generally eat with their mouths closed. Our hardest challenge now is to keep them sitting down at the table during a meal. They always want to get up for some reason. It's fine if they want to get more food or milk, but not if they want to get a toy or start looking around for some miscellaneous object. And they need to ask us before they leave the table. They like to just take their plates up to the counter and dash, but we remind them that they need to get our permission first, especially when we want to continue visiting with them and discussing certain issues. Dinner is especially important for our family and we try to eat together most nights of the week, so this is our time to visit.

At restaurants I now try to get them to put their napkins on their laps. When I tried this when they were younger, it was just a frustrating experience because the napkins would inevitably slip off their laps onto the floor. They wouldn't let me tuck the napkins into their pants to keep them in place. Now that they're getting older I'm trying to get them to learn how to keep the napkin on their lap. We haven't gone over the details for very fancy dining, like complicated place settings and such, but we will when they get older. We do tell them the importance of table manners and that it will always help them in business since there will be business lunches and dinners they'll attend and they'll want to make a good impression in front of their bosses, colleagues and clients, not to mention parents of future girlfriends when they're invited over for dinner.

Drugs, Alcohol and Smoking

We're lucky – our school has a program called DARE for all the fifth graders. A police officer teaches them a class twice a week about the dangers of drugs, alcohol, tobacco and also talks about issues such as bullying and internet safety. The goal is to teach the students how to resist bad influences, build self-esteem and stand up for themselves. This officer also shows up at school at various times and really tries to build a good rapport with the students, so they will feel comfortable coming to him if they have any problems. As a parent, this makes me feel grateful that they have someone other than us and their teachers telling them to stay away from these dangers. I'm also glad they get exposed to it at this age because they're getting this information before they start getting more dangerous messages of what is "cool" and to not listen to or respect authority. It also provides us with an opportunity to discuss what they learn each DARE day.

David and I did use these opportunities to discuss specific drugs and what they do to your body and why they're so bad for you. We discussed how drugs and tobacco can get you addicted very quickly – and that for some drugs, it can happen with the first use. We discussed how alcohol in moderation is OK when you become an adult and that it shouldn't be consumed until then because a person's body and more importantly, brain, are still developing. Our children see us drink wine with dinner or have a cocktail at a restaurant and we explain that a couple of drinks are OK but you don't want to get drunk. I'm hoping that since they feel comfortable discussing these issues with us and asking us questions that it will keep the lines of communication open when situations become trickier in the future. I also hope that all this information puts a negative bias strongly in their minds before they are exposed to tempting situations.

Dick and Jane Moment

The mornings after Dick and Jane would have friends over, I would go into the living room and practice smoking with used cigarette butts sitting in ashtrays and pretend I was drinking with the empty glasses on the coffee table. I felt so grown-up.

Getting Rid of the "Gimmes"

It seems as though my sons have developed a bad case of the "gimmes". They always want new Lego sets, new computer games, new whatever they see on TV or hear about through their friends. It gets so bad that sometimes they want to go to the store to buy a new toy a week after they have received one. David and I have talked extensively about this and feel that they don't value enough what they do have. They are developing a sense of entitlement that is becoming troubling. We don't want them to grow up feeling entitled to get anything they want whenever they want it. We want them to be grateful for what they do have and not take it for granted. We also want to teach them that their comfortable lives are not what everyone experiences.

Like many parents, we always wanted to give our children many opportunities. We focused mainly on giving them experiences that would enrich them and also to introduce them to different activities, so they could decide what their interests were. They have tried all kinds of sports and activities like soccer, tennis, swimming, softball, basketball, tae kwon do, guitar lessons, cello lessons, violin lessons, acting lessons, etc. We've also tried to broaden their horizons with different trips like taking them skiing, river rafting, going to Yosemite, Hawaii, the desert, etc.

David and I have talked to the boys about how fortunate they are and the fact that not everyone is so fortunate. I feel, though, that it goes in one ear and out the other - it just doesn't sink in. So, I've been thinking about what I could do to try to SHOW the boys what we are trying to teach them. I remember visiting orphanages near Tijuana, Mexico when I was 13. That trip changed my view of the world and left a deep impression on me. However, I'm not willing to take my sons down to Mexico to show them poverty because of the dangers the drug war has produced. Trying to show them images of poverty, like on TV or the internet, doesn't get through because they can't really relate to it. I realized that there are examples of people struggling to get by in our own community and if I could show this to my sons, hopefully they can relate to it better. So, I decided that we would donate food to a local food bank in our city that serves about 500 families per month.

I collected a box of food, then brought the boys with me to the food bank. I explained to them that some families don't have enough money to eat three meals a day, even in our community, which is in an affluent area. I talked to the boys about how they would feel if they couldn't eat three meals a day, let alone having snacks. Then when we dropped the food off, I asked if we could look through the warehouse so they could really get a feel for how they were collecting and distributing food to needy families. One of the most impressionable sights we saw were shopping carts that the families come to get. They can come once per month and the cart has a box and a couple of bags of food and one bread item. As we went home, we talked about how that was not a lot of food for a family for a month.

I think actually seeing everything helped make these ideas sink in. Only time will tell. It was definitely very different than just bringing in canned goods to school during food drives. That's a very useful thing to do, mind you, but there isn't much of an emotional tie to it. To see what these families are actually getting and to see that some of the shelves of the food bank are getting low on food really brings home the point that there is a real need right in our own backyard.

Teach Your Boys How to Treat Women and Your Girls How They Should Be Treated

When you're raising boys, you need to teach them how to be respectful of women and how to relate to them for the wellbeing of their future relationships. Your husband can be a big help with this by showing your boys every day how they should treat a woman. If you're not married, it's great if there's a male role model who can teach them this. They need to learn that women are intelligent, strong and independent and that they should be treated with respect and not merely looked upon as objects of affection or otherwise.

Conversely, if you are raising girls, you need to teach them about how they should expect to be treated. Again, your husband or a male role model can be very important in teaching this. Girls need to learn to respect themselves and have a healthy self esteem. They have to be taught that they need to be treated with respect, or they should no longer spend time with the other person.

I was recently talking to another mom, who happens to have a daughter, and she was telling me that some of her daughter's friends told her daughter not to say "no" to a boy or she wouldn't be popular! No, no, no! My friend and I were shocked! Now, these girls were just talking about accepting an invitation to go to lunch, but they have just entered their teen years and if they feel this way now and don't have someone to teach them how terribly incorrect that is, they can get into a lot of trouble in the future. And we need to teach boys not to pressure girls – when they say "no", it means no.

As they continue to get older and get into the dating scene, you can teach them certain nuances of being in a relationship. I hope that my sons will continue to communicate questions and concerns to me so I can help them with my perspective and experience. However, I will still impart advice and values, even if they don't ask for them, hoping that it will seep in somehow as they grow.

Them Teaching You

Changeling

Becoming a mother has changed me in some profound ways. Here are some of these:

- I'm much more social than I ever used to be. I've always tended to be shy since childhood (some people who know me now will be surprised to hear this). Being with a group of people would sometimes make me feel uneasy. Now, however, I have a much easier time starting conversations and being sociable. When you're talking to other parents, you have things in common right away so there are always topics to discuss.

- I'm much bolder than I ever used to be. Probably inherent with the shy tendency was unease with any type of conflict. I don't currently relish conflict, but I don't shrink away from it the way I used to. I stand up for what I believe in and speak up when I need to, especially when it is any circumstance having to do with the boys. I compare it to a mother bear – when it comes to protecting my children, I have no fear.

- My priorities have realigned. I see the big picture clearer now. I really care about the future in a much more personal way because my children's futures have a real stake in it. I don't care about superficial things as much as I used to because now I'm more focused on making sure Zach and Alex are safe and will grow up healthy, happy, with a good education, lots of opportunities and living in a world whose resources and living things are protected and treasured.

- I've finally grown up. I now know what matters and what doesn't (at least to me).

- I try to take better care of myself because I want to live to be a ripe old age to watch Zach and Alex and their future families get older and cross various milestones.

- I will never again believe that housewives ('50's term) ever have any time to sit around and watch soap operas and eat bonbons.

- I now truly understand what unconditional love is. I still sometimes look at one of my boys and have my breath get taken away from how much love I feel for them. I am so proud of them for the individuals they are.

- When I hear a baby crying uncontrollably or a young child having a tantrum, I no longer think "Jeesh, why can't you get your child to be quiet?" I now think, "I'm glad that's not me – this time, at least."

- When something happens to a child, I am more deeply disturbed by it. I feel awful for the child and feel so much empathy for the parents. It's made me care much more for those around me. Additionally, I'm more patient and sometimes remind myself that a certain person is someone else's child, even if it's an adult. That gives me more compassion with people.

Expanding Interests

I really like *Harry Potter*! I know I wouldn't know much about it without children. But I started to read the *Harry Potter* series to the boys before bed and I got sucked into it. After finishing each book, we would then rent the corresponding movie for popcorn night. I look forward to reading the next book in the series after I finish each one. Also, I got to know *Star Wars* a lot more than I would have on my own and I became very well versed on all the different characters and with which number movie(s) they were associated with. When they were smaller, I learned about the names of different trucks. Not that I had a special interest in trucks, mind you, but when you read a book about them over and over again, you're bound to learn the different names and what they do.

This is an aspect of motherhood that I particularly enjoy and look forward to continuing. As the boys develop their interests, I am exposed to them and sometimes find that I enjoy them also. I am exposed to things that I never would be on my own, especially because I have boys. Examples of other interests I have now because of the boys, or at least more of a knowledge of, are swimming, soccer, basketball, rock music and guitar. I like how my sons are continually expanding my world and my interests and keep looking forward to it continuing in the future.

Expectations

We probably all come into parenthood with some expectations of what it will be like. Then we're completely caught off-guard when reality doesn't match. For example, I thought breastfeeding would be fairly easy and a nice, cozy, bonding experience between me and my baby – I mean it's the most natural thing in the world, right? Instead it was an utterly frustrating experience for my babies as well as me.

Zach would cry with frustration and hunger, not being able to get the nourishment he needed and I was crying with frustration and disappointment that I wasn't able to provide it to him. I had nurses and lactation coaches trying to help but my body was still sick after childbirth and just couldn't produce milk. I finally had to give up and bottle-feed. I then tried to breast-feed Alex, but when it again wasn't working, I gave up and gave him the bottle too. It was a disappointing experience with both my sons, but I then just focused on cuddling with them while feeding them a bottle.

I thought that babies slept a lot and were cuddly, cute and fairly quiet most of the time. Then my first-born had colic for six straight months. If he was not sleeping or eating, he was screaming at the top of his lungs – I'm not kidding. Gone were thoughts of leisurely taking him in a stroller through the park or a mall. I was a shut-in during most of this time.

As the boys got older, I looked forward to things like watching Sunday football while munching on fun snacks I prepared. But the boys weren't interested in watching football. I would even make the snacks to coax them, but then they would take some snacks upstairs and watch their favorite shows.

One thing I couldn't have expected or been prepared for is how completely and significantly parenthood changes you. It just kicks you in the shins and gets all your priorities in order. Now I have two small human beings counting on me and I have an awesome responsibility and privilege to help guide them into adulthood. Superficial things just don't matter so much any more and life issues take on so much more significance. You also learn quickly to become much less selfish. The love and concern you have for these small beings far outweighs any old selfish desires. This doesn't mean you miraculously become a saint and lose all flaws, but you do weigh your decisions differently.

Seeing the World Through Their Eyes

This is one of the best parts of being a parent. You sometimes get glimpses of the world through their eyes and see some of the magic they see and believe in. Here are a few of the ways I would get happily caught up in this:

- Reading nursery rhymes at bedtime – I would hear the stories and see the characters the way a child does. Everything seems happy and safe and organized. It would feel cozy in the room and feel like everyone was tucked away safely in bed, comfortable and ready to snooze off into dreamland.

- Watching some of their shows – I wouldn't be able to watch *Sesame Street* on my own, but with my boys sitting next to me, I could see how it was entertaining and educational, too. I could get into the feeling of everyone getting along and seeing things through rose-colored glasses – it's a nice way to view the world.

- Reading books to them – I loved *James and the Giant Peach.* I would get into the story and the characters and want to know what would happen next. I also enjoyed the *Harry Potter* series, especially the early books. I liked how things were magical and full of wonder.

- Watching movies with them – like the shows, there were movies I wouldn't normally watch, but thoroughly enjoyed watching them with the boys and watching their reactions to the stories. A couple of these movies were the *Land Before Time* series, *The Aristocrats*, *Spirit* and *Finding Nemo*.

- Going to an amusement park, like Disneyland – this will really bring out the kid in you. You see your children feeling really excited and running around and you get caught up in their excitement. Also, you go on rides you haven't been on since you were a child and get to remember how thrilling it was for you.

- Watching fireworks or even just the night sky – of course, fireworks are very exciting for children and I got much more pleasure out of viewing them when I was with my children. But even just looking up at the night sky and trying to pick out constellations (which I'm awful at), was fun and full of wonder. It's cool to see how many stars there are and how vast the universe is – it puts our problems and concerns into perspective.

You Never Stop Being a Mom

Looking to the Future

I can't help but do this, although I do try to stay in the moment as much as possible because I know that's how to best enjoy the time I have with my family. But I look at my sons and I see how far they've come. They're getting to the age where I can see the men they will become. Their features are manlier and their personalities, strengths and interests have become more developed. I realize I will need to begin to teach them skills to become independent young men, like cooking, laundry, balancing checkbooks, etc.

I also think about them going into high school and then college and leaving home either during college or shortly after. I get sad and sentimental at these times, realizing that the amount of time I have left with them living with us is preciously short. I've already told them (tongue-in-cheek, but not completely) that if they live away from home during college, they can come visit whenever and as often as they want and I'll cook their favorite foods and do their laundry for them. I know that might sound awful to some of you, but I'm humorously bribing them to come and visit as often as possible by making it worth their while.

I also think about how they'll be in relationships down the road and how important their girlfriends will be to them. I hope I get along with their future girlfriends and know I need to try to hold my tongue if I don't. Eventually, they'll probably get married and hopefully have children. I hope I like their future wives and I will really try to. I've already told them that we will happily babysit their children.

My parents were always very involved in Zach's and Alex's lives and regularly babysat them from the very beginning. Because of this, they've always had a very close relationship with them and knew their personalities and what they were into as they grew. I want that kind of relationship with my future grandchildren and want to be able to be an integral part of their lives from the very beginning. I know for that to happen, we need to make it beneficial for the parents by letting them take a break routinely and respecting their parenting rules, so they always feel comfortable with us babysitting.

As I look to the future and the inevitability of an empty nest, it reminds me that I need to make sure I have my own life, beyond being a mother. So, I try to expand my horizons now and build more hobbies for myself. I get sad thinking about an empty nest, but I try to also see the opportunities it might provide. We will have much more freedom and can take impromptu trips. I can have quiet in the house when I want and my schedule will be more flexible. I also realize that we will get used to it and that if we have built a solid foundation with our sons, we will still be a part of their ever-expanding, growing lives.

Reflecting on the Past

And in looking to the future, I inevitably find myself looking back to the past. When I see young children playing outside, walking around the neighborhood or playing in the park, I remember Zach and Alex when they were that age. I remember taking them to the park and I remember being right behind them when they were climbing up the equipment when they were very young and prone to falling. I remember them first learning to ride bikes, use skates, skateboards, throw balls, kick balls, swing a bat, etc. I remember the toys that were their favorites at different ages and the shows and movies that were their favorites. I remember each grade they were in, their teachers and their friends. I remember taking them to birthday parties and throwing their own birthday parties. I remember taking them to all their sports practices and watching almost all their games.

We are now getting to the point where some of the things we've always done with the boys will be ending. For our last Easter, we dyed eggs and wondered if this would be the last time they wanted to. We are currently planning Zach's 13th birthday party. He has already mentioned that this may be his last party because he's getting too old for them – we will always have some type of celebration for the boys, but maybe not actual parties. I'm already wondering how Halloween will play out this year. We've always walked with them for trick-or-treating and last year, hung back a bit but were still there. Will that be the case this year or do we just let them go by themselves?

I'm a bit sad every time I realize that this might be the last time we do some type of event with them. But I try to remind myself that we have been very involved in their lives and enjoyed our time with them the whole time they were growing up. So at least I don't feel like David and I missed out on anything. We spent time with Zach and Alex and had fun with holidays, birthdays, vacations, weekends, Friday popcorn nights, etc. I hope the boys will remember all the fun things we did together. Now as I look to the past, I can't help but also look to the future and hope I'll be able to re-live some of these experiences with grandchildren (eventually)! Looking to the past, looking to the future – somehow it all gets inter-connected.

www.ingramcontent.com/pod-product-compliance
Lightning Source LLC
Chambersburg PA
CBHW051508030726
47592CB00006B/2157